지식이
감동이 되는 책!

세상이 아무리 바쁘게 돌아가더라도
책까지 아무렇게나 빨리 만들 수는 없습니다.
어머니가 손수 지어주는 밥처럼
정성이 듬뿍 담긴 건강한 책을 만들고 싶습니다.

길벗스쿨은 쉽게 배우고 깨쳐 공부에 자신감을 주는 책,
재미와 감동으로 마음을 풍요롭게 해 주는 책으로
독자 여러분께 다가가겠습니다.

아이의 꿈을 키워 주는 정성을
지금, 만나보세요.

미리 책을 읽고 따라해본 2만 베타테스터 여러분과
무따기 체험단, 길벗스쿨 엄마 2% 기획단,
시나공 평가단, 토익 배틀, 대학생 기자단까지!
믿을 수 있는 책을 함께 만들어주신 독자 여러분께 감사드립니다.

홈페이지의 '독자마당'에 오시면
책을 함께 만들 수 있습니다.

(주)도서출판 길벗 www.gilbut.co.kr
길벗 이지톡 www.eztok.co.kr
길벗스쿨 www.gilbutschool.co.kr

미국교과서 핵심 리딩 100

2

TinyFolds 지음

길벗스쿨

저자 TinyFolds
기본을 중요시하는 교육정신을 바탕으로 유아에서 성인에 이르는 영어 학습자를 위한
다양한 영역의 수준 높은 영어 교육 콘텐츠를 제공합니다.

– 유아 영어리딩 프로그램 RollingPin 프로그램 개발
– 한솔교육, 웅진씽크빅, 이퓨처, 대교, Learn 21, 쎄듀북스, 비상교육 등 영어 프로젝트 진행 및 교재 개발

미국교과서 핵심 리딩 100 ❷
American Textbook Core Topics 100 ❷

초판 발행 · 2021년 1월 15일

지은이 · TinyFolds
발행인 · 이종원
발행처 · 길벗스쿨
출판사 등록일 · 2006년 7월 1일
주소 · 서울시 마포구 월드컵로 10길 56(서교동)
대표 전화 · 02)332-0931 | **팩스** · 02)323-0586
홈페이지 · www.gilbutschool.co.kr | **이메일** · gilbutschool@gilbut.co.kr

기획 및 책임 편집 · 김남희(sophia@gilbut.co.kr) | **본문 디자인** · 신세진 | **제작** · 이진혁
영업마케팅 · 김진성, 박선경 | **웹마케팅** · 박달님, 권은나 | **영업관리** · 정경화 | **독자지원** · 송혜란, 홍혜진

편집진행 · 김현정 | **전산편집** · 연디자인 | **표지 디자인** · 박찬진 | **영문감수** · Ryan P. Lagace
사진 · shutterstock.com, commons.wikimedia.org | **인쇄** · 두경 m&p | **제본** · 경문제책 | **녹음** · 와이알미디어

ISBN 979-11-6406-293-5 64740
(길벗 도서번호 30472)

정가 15,000원

독자의 1초를 아껴주는 정성 길벗출판사
길벗 | IT실용서, IT/일반 수험서, IT전문서, 경제실용서, 취미실용서, 건강실용서, 자녀교육서
더퀘스트 | 인문교양서, 비즈니스서
길벗이지톡 | 어학단행본, 어학수험서
길벗스쿨 | 국어학습서, 수학학습서, 유아학습서, 어린이교양서, 어학학습서, 교과서

길벗스쿨 공식 카페 〈기적의 공부방〉 · cafe.naver.com/gilbutschool
인스타그램 / 카카오플러스친구 · @gilbutschool

미국 초등학교 교과서에서 엄선한 100개의 교과 지식을 읽으며
논픽션 리딩에 자신감을 키워요!

〈미국 교과서 핵심 리딩 100〉 시리즈는 미국 초등학교 주요 과목에서 꼭 다루는 100개의 필수 주제만을 엄선하여 한국 초등 고학년 수준에 맞는 문장으로 구성한 리딩 학습서입니다. 지문을 읽고 문제로 바로 확인하는 간결한 호흡으로 설계하여 논픽션 지문에 익숙하지 않은 학생이라도 혼자서 무리 없이 학습을 이어 나갈 수 있도록 했습니다. 다양한 영역의 100가지 교과 지식을 꾸준히 읽다 보면 배경지식이 쌓이는 것은 물론, 이미 알고 있는 교과 지식도 영어로 확장시켜 저절로 리딩 실력이 향상됨을 느낄 수 있을 것입니다.

★Features

●독해력과 교과 지식을 동시에 잡는 미국교과서

과학, 사회, 수학, 문학 등 미국 초등 교과서의 필수 학습 주제를 뽑아 구성한 100개 지문을 읽으며 리딩의 기틀을 마련하고 교과 및 배경지식을 습득할 수 있습니다.

●다양한 주제글을 정확하고 빠르게 읽는 '집중 리딩' 학습

읽으면서 중심 내용을 바로 이해하고, 다양한 유형의 문제를 풀며 새로 얻은 정보까지 완벽히 소화하게 하는 '집중 리딩' 설계로 단기간에 독해력을 향상시킬 수 있습니다.

●다양한 학습 장치를 통한 효과적인 읽기 훈련

지문 요약, 도표 완성 활동으로 글의 구성을 파악하는 리딩스킬과 단어 활용 능력이 향상됩니다. 지문의 핵심 내용을 정리하는 활동을 하면서 초등 고학년 시기에 갖춰야 하는 통합적 사고력 훈련까지 할 수 있습니다.

How to Study This Book

★1단계★ 지문 들어보기

제목과 그림을 통해 내용을 대략적으로 추측해 본 후 원어민의 발음으로 지문 내용을 들으며 중심 내용을 파악해 봅니다.

★2단계★ 리딩 지문 읽기

음원을 들으며 대략적으로 파악한 내용을 지문을 꼼꼼히 읽으면서 자세히 파악합니다. 의미를 몰라 독해가 막히는 부분은 **Words to Know** 상자의 어휘 설명을 참고합니다.

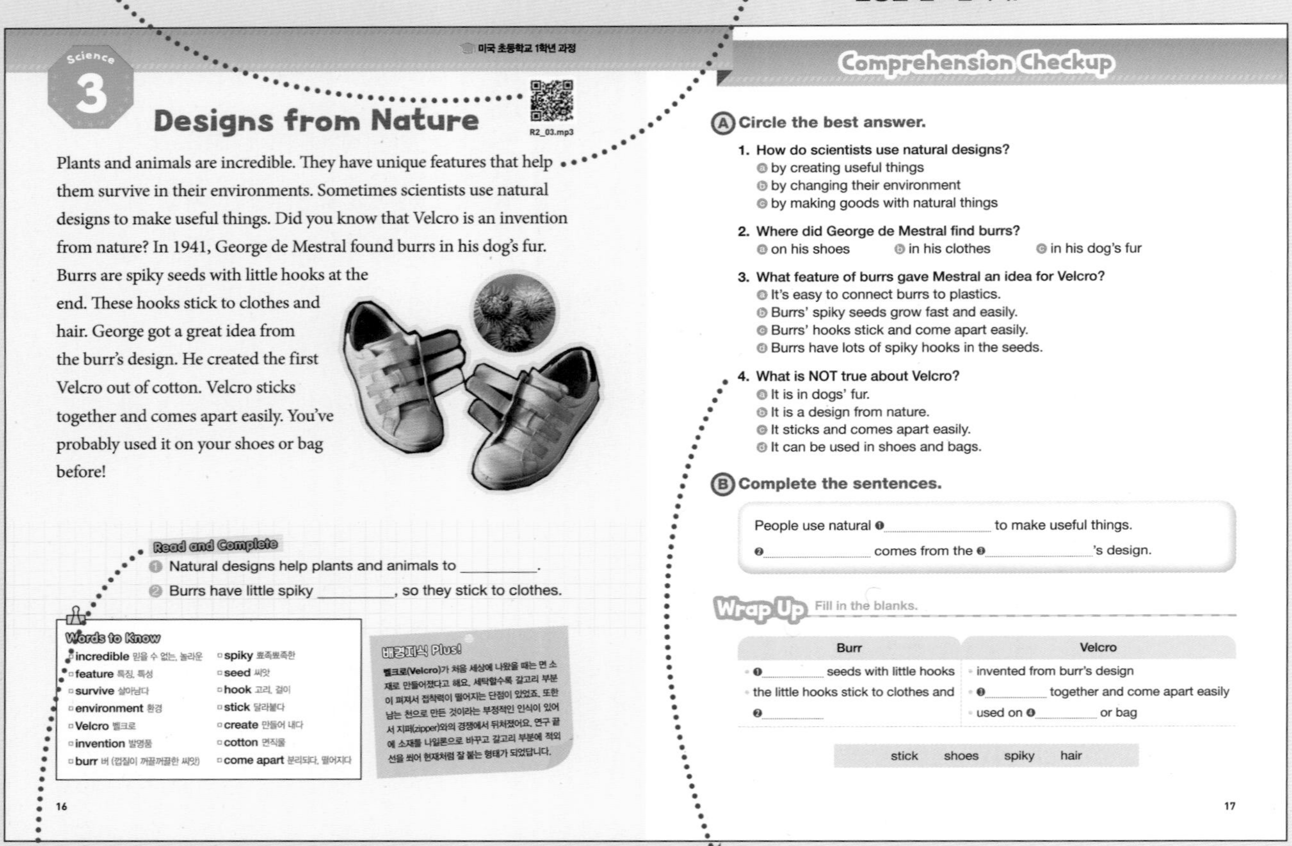

미국 초등학교 1학년 과정

Science 3

Designs from Nature

R2_03.mp3

Plants and animals are incredible. They have unique features that help them survive in their environments. Sometimes scientists use natural designs to make useful things. Did you know that Velcro is an invention from nature? In 1941, George de Mestral found burrs in his dog's fur. Burrs are spiky seeds with little hooks at the end. These hooks stick to clothes and hair. George got a great idea from the burr's design. He created the first Velcro out of cotton. Velcro sticks together and comes apart easily. You've probably used it on your shoes or bag before!

Read and Complete

1. Natural designs help plants and animals to ________.
2. Burrs have little spiky ________, so they stick to clothes.

Words to Know

- incredible 믿을 수 없는, 놀라운
- feature 특징, 특성
- survive 살아남다
- environment 환경
- Velcro 벨크로
- invention 발명품
- burr 버 (껍질이 까끌까끌한 씨앗)
- spiky 뾰족뾰족한
- seed 씨앗
- hook 고리, 걸이
- stick 달라붙다
- create 만들어 내다
- cotton 면직물
- come apart 분리되다, 떨어지다

배경지식 Plus!

벨크로(Velcro)가 처음 세상에 나왔을 때는 면 소재로 만들어졌다고 해요. 세탁할수록 갈고리 부분이 퍼져서 접착력이 떨어지는 단점이 있었죠. 또한 남는 천으로 만든 것이라는 부정적인 인식이 있어서 지퍼(zipper)와의 경쟁에서 뒤처졌어요. 연구 끝에 소재를 나일론으로 바꾸고 갈고리 부분에 적외선을 쐬어 현재처럼 잘 붙는 형태가 되었답니다.

16

Comprehension Checkup

Ⓐ Circle the best answer.

1. How do scientists use natural designs?
   ⓐ by creating useful things
   ⓑ by changing their environment
   ⓒ by making goods with natural things
2. Where did George de Mestral find burrs?
   ⓐ on his shoes ⓑ in his clothes ⓒ in his dog's fur
3. What feature of burrs gave Mestral an idea for Velcro?
   ⓐ It's easy to connect burrs to plastics.
   ⓑ Burrs' spiky seeds grow fast and easily.
   ⓒ Burrs' hooks stick and come apart easily.
   ⓓ Burrs have lots of spiky hooks in the seeds.
4. What is NOT true about Velcro?
   ⓐ It is in dogs' fur.
   ⓑ It is a design from nature.
   ⓒ It sticks and comes apart easily.
   ⓓ It can be used in shoes and bags.

Ⓑ Complete the sentences.

People use natural ❶________ to make useful things.
❷________ comes from the ❸________'s design.

Wrap Up Fill in the blanks.

Burr	Velcro
❶________ seeds with little hooks	invented from burr's design
the little hooks stick to clothes and ❷________	❸________ together and come apart easily
	used on ❹________ or bag

stick shoes spiky hair

17

★3단계★ 대략적 내용 확인 및 배경지식 확장하기

핵심 단어를 짚으며 문장을 완성하는 **Read and Complete** 문제로 지문의 전체적인 이해도를 확인합니다. QR코드를 찍어 중요 어휘의 소리를 확인하고, 그 의미를 지문에서 찾아 다시 확인합니다. **배경지식 Plus!** 코너를 통해 더 넓은 범위의 교과 지식을 얻어갈 수 있습니다.

★4단계★ 다양한 형식의 문제를 풀며 독해력 다지기

Ⓐ 객관식 4문항을 풀면서 지문을 얼마나 정확하게 이해했는지 확인합니다. 막연한 이해를 넘어 지문 내용을 내 것으로 만드는 힘을 길러줍니다.

Ⓑ 지문 전체의 내용을 짧게 요약합니다. 지문을 요약해서 다시 써 보는 훈련을 통해 글의 핵심을 파악하고, 긴 글을 줄여서 표현하는 능력이 생깁니다.

Wrap Up 지문 내용을 글의 성격에 따라 다양한 형태로 시각화하여 정리하는 활동을 통해 단어 활용 능력을 기릅니다.

MP3 듣기
도서 페이지의 '자료실'을 터치하면 MP3 파일을 바로 듣거나 전체 다운로드를 할 수 있습니다.

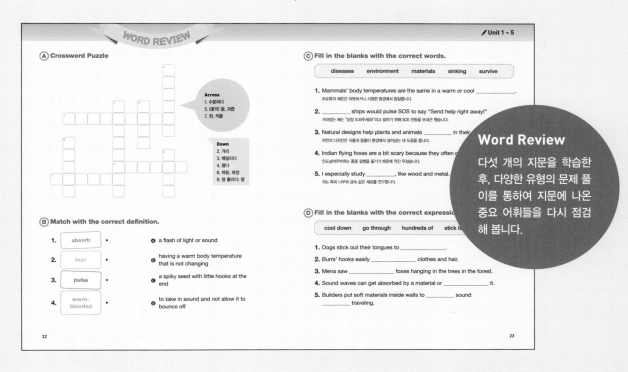

Word Review
다섯 개의 지문을 학습한 후, 다양한 유형의 문제 풀이를 통하여 지문에 나온 중요 어휘들을 다시 점검해 봅니다.

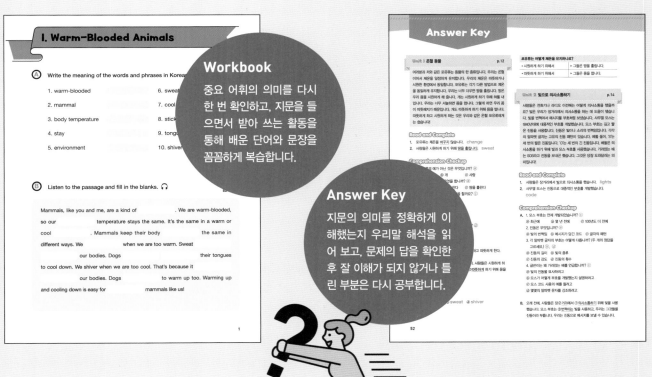

Workbook
중요 어휘의 의미를 다시 한 번 확인하고, 지문을 들으면서 받아 쓰는 활동을 통해 배운 단어와 문장을 꼼꼼하게 복습합니다.

Answer Key
지문의 의미를 정확하게 이해했는지 우리말 해석을 읽어 보고, 문제의 답을 확인한 후 잘 이해가 되지 않거나 틀린 부분은 다시 공부합니다.

Table of Contents

Science

Social Studies

Language Arts, Art, Music, Math

제안하는 스케줄대로 공부하면 두 달 동안 미국교과서 핵심 리딩 100 1,2권의
학습을 모두 끝낼 수 있습니다. 학습한 날의 날짜를 기록하세요.

Day 1	Day 2	Day 3	Day 4	Day 5
Unit 1 Unit 2　　/	Unit 3 Unit 4　　/	Unit 5 Review 1　　/	Unit 6 Unit 7　　/	Unit 8 Unit 9　　/
Day 6	**Day 7**	**Day 8**	**Day 9**	**Day 10**
Unit 10 Review 2　　/	Unit 11 Unit 12　　/	Unit 13 Unit 14　　/	Unit 15 Review 3　　/	Unit 16 Unit 17　　/
Day 11	Day 12	Day 13	Day 14	Day 15
Unit 18 Unit 19　　/	Unit 20 Review 4　　/	Unit 21 Unit 22　　/	Unit 23 Unit 24　　/	Unit 25 Review 5　　/
Day 16	**Day 17**	**Day 18**	**Day 19**	**Day 20**
Unit 26 Unit 27　　/	Unit 28 Unit 29　　/	Unit 30 Review 6　　/	Unit 31 Unit 32　　/	Unit 33 Unit 34　　/
Day 21	**Day 22**	**Day 23**	**Day 24**	**Day 25**
Unit 35 Review 7　　/	Unit 36 Unit 37　　/	Unit 38 Unit 39　　/	Unit 40 Review 8　　/	Unit 41 Unit 42　　/
Day 26	**Day 27**	**Day 28**	**Day 29**	**Day 30**
Unit 43 Unit 44　　/	Unit 45 Review 9　　/	Unit 46 Unit 47　　/	Unit 48 Unit 49　　/	Unit 50 Review 10　　/

R2_01.mp3

Warm-Blooded Animals

Mammals, like you and me, are a kind of animal. We are warm-blooded, so our body temperature stays the same. It's the same in a warm or cool environment. Mammals keep their body temperatures the same in different ways. We sweat when we are too warm. Sweat cools down our bodies. Dogs stick out their tongues to cool down. We shiver when we are too cool. That's because it warms up our bodies. Dogs shiver to warm up too. Warming up and cooling down is easy for warm-blooded mammals like us!

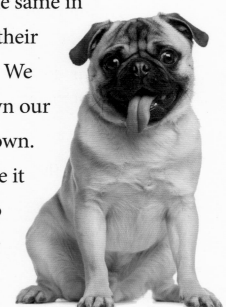

Read and Complete

1 Mammals don't _____ their body temperatures.

2 People _____ to cool down.

Words to Know

□ **warm-blooded** 온혈의
□ **mammal** 포유동물
□ **body temperature** 체온
□ **stay** 머무르다, 계속 있다
□ **environment** 환경
□ **sweat** 땀을 흘리다; 땀

□ **cool down** 시원하게 하다
□ **stick out** ~을 내밀다
□ **tongue** 혀
□ **shiver** (몸을) 떨다
□ **warm up** 따뜻하게 하다

배경지식 Plus!

개들의 평균 체온(body temperature)은 체구와 나이에 따라 차이는 있지만 보통 사람보다 높은 38.5℃ 정도라고 해요. 더위에 취약한 개들은 입을 벌리고 혀를 내밀어 호흡하여 침이 증발하며 발생하는 기화열로 체온을 내려요. 이때 코로도 호흡하는데 콧속에 많은 미세한 혈관들이 코를 통과하는 공기와 열을 교환해서 체온을 내리기도 하지요.

Ⓐ Circle the best answer.

1. What is not an example of a mammal?
ⓐ fish　　　　　ⓑ dog　　　　　ⓒ human

2. What do humans do when they are cold?
ⓐ shiver　　　　ⓑ sleep　　　　ⓒ sweat

3. What will dogs do in a hot environment?
ⓐ They will shiver.
ⓑ They will sweat.
ⓒ They will stick out their tongues.
ⓓ They will change their body temperature.

4. What is NOT true about mammals?
ⓐ They are warm-blooded.
ⓑ They are a kind of animal.
ⓒ They keep their body temperatures the same.
ⓓ They all cool down and warm up the same way.

Ⓑ Complete the sentences.

Mammals keep their body temperatures the ❶＿＿＿＿＿＿＿＿. People sweat to cool down. Also, they shiver to ❷＿＿＿＿＿＿＿ up.

Wrap Up Fill in the blanks.

How do mammals keep their ❶＿＿＿＿ temperatures?	
• to ❷＿＿＿＿ down	▸ They ❸＿＿＿＿.
• to warm up	▸ They ❹＿＿＿＿.

sweat　　cool　　shiver　　body

R2_02.mp3

Science 2
Communicating with Lights

How did people communicate before phones and radio? Lights helped us communicate over long distances. Flashing a light sent messages as a code. Samuel Morse developed a popular code in the 1840s. Morse code uses long and short pulses. A pulse is a flash of light or sound. Each letter of the alphabet has its own pulse pattern. For example, "S" is three short pulses. "O" is three long pulses. Ships used lights and Morse code to communicate. Sinking ships would pulse SOS. That means to send help right away!

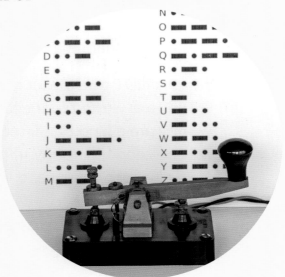

Read and Complete

❶ People communicated over long distances with _____.

❷ Samuel Morse developed a popular _____ with pulses.

Words to Know

□ **communicate** 소통하다
□ **distance** 거리
□ **flash** 비추다; 번쩍임
□ **message** 메시지
□ **code** 암호, 부호, 코드
□ **develop** 개발하다
□ **popular** 인기 있는, 대중적인
□ **pulse** (광선·음향 등의) 진동, 파동
□ **pattern** (정형화된) 패턴, 양식
□ **sink** 가라앉다

배경피식 Plus!

모스 부호(Morse code)는 길고 짧은 전류로 전신 기호를 만들어 소통하는 체계입니다. 우리나라 한글의 전신 부호가 만들어진 때는 1890년대라고 해요. 통신 기술이 발달한 오늘날에도 위급한 상황에서는 여전히 전신 부호가 가장 기초적인 비상 소통수단으로 쓰이고 있어요. 〈엑시트〉, 〈기생충〉과 같은 영화에도 전신 부호를 사용하는 장면들이 나온답니다.

(A) Circle the best answer.

1. When was Morse code developed?
   ⓐ recently   ⓑ a few years ago   ⓒ over 100 years ago

2. What is a pulse?
   ⓐ a flash of light   ⓑ a code with messages   ⓒ a pattern of a letter

3. How does a code of each alphabet letter differ? (Choose 2 answers.)
   ⓐ length of pulses   ⓑ types of lights
   ⓒ strength of pulses   ⓓ number of pulses

4. Why does the writer mention sinking ships?
   ⓐ to describe pulses of lights
   ⓑ to explain how Morse developed codes
   ⓒ to give an example of using Morse code
   ⓓ to emphasize some letters of the alphabet

(B) Complete the sentences.

A long time ago, people used lights to ❶_____ over long ❷_____. Morse code uses ❸_____ lights and we call them pulses. We can send message with pulses.

Wrap Up   Fill in the blanks.

Morse code		
용도	• to communicate over ❶_____ distances	
방법	• using a ❷_____ of light as a pulse	
	• making ❸_____ letters with long and short ❹_____ patterns	

long
alphabet
flash
pulse

Science 3

Designs from Nature

R2_03.mp3

Plants and animals are incredible. They have unique features that help them survive in their environments. Sometimes scientists use natural designs to make useful things. Did you know that Velcro is an invention from nature? In 1941, George de Mestral found burrs in his dog's fur. Burrs are spiky seeds with little hooks at the end. These hooks stick to clothes and hair. George got a great idea from the burr's design. He created the first Velcro out of cotton. Velcro sticks together and comes apart easily. You've probably used it on your shoes or bag before!

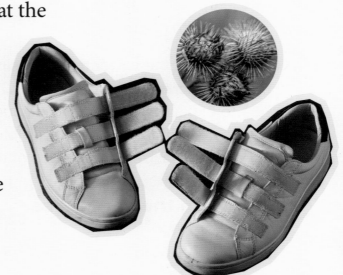

Read and Complete

① Natural designs help plants and animals to _____.

② Burrs have little spiky _____, so they stick to clothes.

Words to Know

- incredible 믿을 수 없는, 놀라운
- feature 특징, 특성
- survive 살아남다
- environment 환경
- Velcro 벨크로
- invention 발명품
- burr 버 (껍질이 꺼끌꺼끌한 씨앗)
- spiky 뾰족뾰족한
- seed 씨앗
- hook 고리, 걸이
- stick 달라붙다
- create 만들어 내다
- cotton 면직물
- come apart 분리되다, 떨어지다

배경지식 Plus!

벨크로(Velcro)가 처음 세상에 나왔을 때는 면 소재로 만들어졌다고 해요. 세탁할수록 갈고리 부분이 펴져서 접착력이 떨어지는 단점이 있었죠. 또한 남는 천으로 만든 것이라는 부정적인 인식이 있어서 지퍼(zipper)와의 경쟁에서 뒤처졌어요. 연구 끝에 소재를 나일론으로 바꾸고 갈고리 부분에 적외선을 쐬어 현재처럼 잘 붙는 형태가 되었답니다.

16

(A) Circle the best answer.

1. How do scientists use natural designs?
- (a) by creating useful things
- (b) by changing their environment
- (c) by making goods with natural things

2. Where did George de Mestral find burrs?
- (a) on his shoes
- (b) in his clothes
- (c) in his dog's fur

3. What feature of burrs gave Mestral an idea for Velcro?
- (a) It's easy to connect burrs to plastics.
- (b) Burrs' spiky seeds grow fast and easily.
- (c) Burrs' hooks stick and come apart easily.
- (d) Burrs have lots of spiky hooks in the seeds.

4. What is NOT true about Velcro?
- (a) It is in dogs' fur.
- (b) It is a design from nature.
- (c) It sticks and comes apart easily.
- (d) It can be used in shoes and bags.

(B) Complete the sentences.

People use natural ❶_____ to make useful things.

❷_____ comes from the ❸_____'s design.

Wrap Up   Fill in the blanks.

Burr	Velcro
• ❶_____ seeds with little hooks	• invented from burr's design
• the little hooks stick to clothes and	• ❸_____ together and come apart easily
❷_____	• used on ❹_____ or bag

stick	shoes	spiky	hair

Indian Flying Foxes

R2_04.mp3

Mena and his father were in the forest outside their village in India. They saw hundreds of foxes hanging in the trees. These foxes had strange, leathery arms. "Father, I'm scared," Mena said. His father smiled and answered, "Those are Indian flying foxes, my son. They are actually a kind of bat. They are a bit scary because they often carry diseases. But they eat only fruit, flowers, and insects. Flying foxes also help pollinate flowers by drinking nectar. So, they are an important part of the environment."

Read and Complete

1 Indian flying foxes live in forests in _____.

2 Indian flying foxes have strange, _____ arms.

Words to Know

□ village 마을
□ hundreds of 수백의 ~
□ hang 매달리다
□ strange 이상한
□ leathery 가죽 같은
□ bat 박쥐
□ a bit 약간
□ disease 질병
□ pollinate 수분하다
　(수술의 꽃가루가 암술로 옮겨지다)
□ nectar (꽃의) 꿀, 과즙

배경지식 Plus!

인도날여우박쥐(Indian flying fox)는 바나나, 망고와 같은 과일을 주식으로 먹어 '큰인도과일박쥐'라고 불리기도 해요. 주로 인도와 방글라데시, 티베트 지역에 분포한답니다. 인도날여우박쥐는 과일이나 꿀을 먹는 과정에서 꽃가루나 씨앗을 옮기고 퍼뜨리는 역할을 한답니다.

Comprehension Checkup

A Circle the best answer.

1. Where did Mena find Indian flying foxes?
　ⓐ in the trees　　ⓑ in his village　　ⓒ near flowers

2. What kind of animal are Indian flying foxes?
　ⓐ a fox　　ⓑ a bat　　ⓒ an insect

3. Why are Indian flying foxes dangerous?
　ⓐ They can carry diseases.　　ⓑ They eat helpful insects.
　ⓒ They fly around villages.　　ⓓ They have strange leathery arms.

4. What is NOT true about Indian flying foxes?
　ⓐ They help pollinate flowers.
　ⓑ They eat fruits and drink nectar.
　ⓒ They are bats, but look like foxes.
　ⓓ They scare people to get food.

B Complete the sentences.

Indian flying foxes are found in India. They may be ❶_____ because they can carry ❷_____. But Indian flying foxes help their environment by ❸_____ flowers.

Wrap Up Fill in the blanks.

Indian Flying Foxes

신체 특징	have strange, ❶_____ arms
위험성	carry ❷_____
장점	help ❸_____ flowers ▸ good for the ❹_____

pollinate

leathery

environment

diseases

19

Science **5**

Sound Travels

R2_05.mp3

I'm a materials engineer. I especially study materials, like wood and metal. I check to see how well they absorb sound. Sound travels in waves. Sound waves can get absorbed by a material or go through it. Soft materials, like fabric, sponge, or cardboard, absorb sounds well. Builders put these materials inside walls to stop sound from traveling. Hard materials, like wood or glass, don't absorb sound well. The sound waves usually bounce off these materials. Builders also use these hard materials to block sound from entering an area.

Read and Complete

① Soft materials _____ sound from traveling.

② _____ materials don't absorb sounds well.

Words to Know

- material 재료, 물질
- engineer 엔지니어, 기술자
- especially 특히
- metal 금속
- absorb 흡수하다
- wave 파동, 파장
- go through 통과하다
- fabric 천, 직물
- cardboard 판지
- stop A from -ing
  A가 ~하는 것을 막다
- bounce off 튕겨 나오다
- block A from -ing
  A가 ~하는 것을 막다
- soundproof
  방음 장치가 되어 있는

배경지식 Plus!

건축을 할 때 소리를 흡수하기 위해 가장 많이 쓰이는 것은 부드러운 소재, 그리고 아주 작은 구멍들이 뚫려 있는 재료들이라고 해요. 음파로 인해 구멍 안의 공기가 진동하고 그로 인해 마찰이 발생하여, 소리 에너지가 열에너지로 바뀌어 재료에 흡수되는 원리예요. 영화관 바닥이나 벽에 카펫 소재 같은 것이 많이 보이는 이유를 이제 알겠죠?

(A) Circle the best answer.

1. Which material absorbs sound well?
- (a) wood
- (b) glass
- (c) sponge

2. How does sound travel?
- (a) in waves
- (b) in materials
- (c) by bouncing

3. How do builders make walls to be soundproof?
- (a) They make walls with soft materials.
- (b) They put soft materials inside walls.
- (c) They make thicker and higher walls.
- (d) They cover walls with fabric or cardboard.

4. What is NOT true about sound waves?
- (a) They bounce off hard materials.
- (b) They can get absorbed by fabrics.
- (c) They go through soft materials.
- (d) Sometimes they are stopped from traveling.

(B) Complete the sentences.

Sound travels in ❶_____. Soft materials ❷_____ sound well. On the other hand, sound waves ❸_____ off hard materials.

Wrap Up Fill in the blanks.

Sound Travels

구분	종류	소리의 이동
❶_____ materials	▸ fabric, sponge, cardboard	▸ ❸_____ sounds well
❷_____ materials	▸ wood, metal, glass	▸ sound waves ❹_____ off these materials

absorb   hard   bounce   soft

21

A Crossword Puzzle

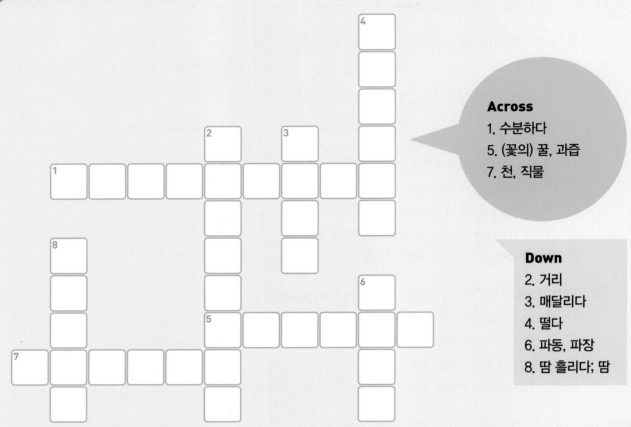

Across
1. 수분하다
5. (꽃의) 꿀, 과즙
7. 천, 직물

Down
2. 거리
3. 매달리다
4. 떨다
6. 파동, 파장
8. 땀 흘리다; 땀

B Match with the correct definition.

1. absorb •

2. burr •

3. pulse •

4. warm-blooded •

ⓐ a flash of light or sound

ⓑ having a warm body temperature that is not changing

ⓒ a spiky seed with little hooks at the end

ⓓ to take in sound and not allow it to bounce off

22

C Fill in the blanks with the correct words.

> diseases   environment   materials   sinking   survive

1. Mammals' body temperatures are the same in a warm or cool _____.
포유류의 체온은 따뜻하거나 시원한 환경에서 동일합니다.

2. _____ ships would pulse SOS to say "Send help right away!"
가라앉는 배는 "당장 도와주세요!"라고 말하기 위해 SOS 진동을 보내곤 했습니다.

3. Natural designs help plants and animals _____ in their environments.
자연의 디자인은 식물과 동물이 환경에서 살아남는 데 도움을 줍니다.

4. Indian flying foxes are a bit scary because they often carry _____.
인도날여우박쥐는 종종 질병을 옮기기 때문에 약간 무섭습니다.

5. I especially study _____, like wood and metal.
저는 특히 나무와 금속 같은 재료를 연구합니다.

D Fill in the blanks with the correct expressions.

> cool down   go through   hundreds of   stick to   stop ~ from

1. Dogs stick out their tongues to _____.

2. Burrs' hooks easily _____ clothes and hair.

3. Mena saw _____ foxes hanging in the trees in the forest.

4. Sound waves can get absorbed by a material or _____ it.

5. Builders put soft materials inside walls to _____ sound _____ traveling.

No More Bees?

R2_06.mp3

Bees are disappearing. Their colonies are collapsing. Scientists think that pesticides are killing millions of bees each year. Farmers use pesticides on food crops to keep insects away. Pesticides are poisonous, and bees are contacting them. They weaken the bees so diseases harm them. Also, pesticides affect the brains of the bees. This causes them to get lost while looking for nectar. When bees travel for nectar, they help pollinate crops. Bees cannot survive alone, and humans wouldn't have very much to eat without bees. We should change how we farm or bees might disappear.

Read and Complete

① Bee _____ are disappearing.

② Pesticides are _____ millions of bees.

Words to Know

- disappear 사라지다
- colony 군집
- collapse 붕괴되다
- pesticide 농약
- millions of 수백만의 ~
- keep A away A를 멀리하다
- poisonous 독이 있는
- contact 접촉하다
- weaken 약화시키다
- harm 해치다
- affect 영향을 미치다
- get lost 길을 잃다

배경지식 Plus!

꿀이 있는 곳을 발견한 꿀벌이 집으로 돌아와서 어떻게 그곳을 동료들에게 알려줄 수 있을까요? 꿀벌은 춤으로 의사소통을 한답니다. 꿀이 집에서 10미터 이내에 있으면 동그라미를 그리는 춤을 추고, 100미터 너머에 있으면 8자를 그리는 춤을 춥니다. 춤의 속도와 지속 시간으로 꿀의 풍요로움 정도를 나타내기도 해요.

(A) Circle the best answer.

1. What do farmers use to protect their crops?
  ⓐ colonies   ⓑ insects   ⓒ pesticides

2. What harms bees?
  ⓐ crops   ⓑ nectar   ⓒ diseases

3. How do pesticides affect bees?
  ⓐ Pesticides remove their food crops.
  ⓑ Pesticides make them stop eating.
  ⓒ Pesticides weaken them and get sick.
  ⓓ Pesticides cause them to contact dangerous crops.

4. What can be inferred from the passage?
  ⓐ Humans should raise more bees.
  ⓑ Bees play important roles in producing crops.
  ⓒ Bees are stealing lots of nectar from humans.
  ⓓ Humans have no choice but to use pesticides.

(B) Complete the sentences.

Pesticides are ❶_____ and make bees get sick. They

❷_____ brains of bees. Then, bees have a hard time to look for

❸_____. Humans must change how they farm.

Wrap Up Fill in the blanks.

Disappearing Bees

Farmers use ❶_____ pesticides.

▸ Bees ❷_____ them and become sick.

▸ The pesticides affect their ❸_____.

▸ It's hard for them to find ❹_____, and they cannot survive.

brains
contact
poisonous
nectar

Explosive Facts!

R2_07.mp3

We live on the Earth's crust, but it is really hot underneath. Under the crust is the mantle. The mantle is made up of hot, red rocks. We call it magma. This magma sometimes comes to the surface. Magma can erupt from volcanoes! We call it lava. Lava can only erupt from active volcanoes. There are over 1,900 active volcanoes on Earth! There are also volcanoes that are not active. They won't erupt for a long time. The other volcanoes are extinct volcanoes, and they will never erupt again.

Read and Complete

❶ It's very hot underneath the Earth's _____.

❷ Magma comes to the surface, and we call it _____.

Words to Know

- □ **explosive** 폭발하기 쉬운
- □ **crust** (지구의) 지각, 표면
- □ **underneath** 아래에
- □ **mantle** (지구의) 맨틀
- □ **be made up of** ~으로 구성되다
- □ **call A B** A를 B라고 부르다
- □ **magma** 마그마
- □ **surface** 표면, 지면
- □ **erupt** 분출하다, 폭발하다
- □ **volcano** 화산
- □ **lava** 용암
- □ **active volcano** 활화산
- □ **extinct volcano** 사화산

배경지식 Plus!

폭발 가능성이 있지만 일정 시간 휴지기를 두고 있는 화산을 '휴화산'이라고 해요. 그렇다면 우리나라의 백두산과 한라산은 활화산, 사화산, 휴화산 중 무엇으로 분류할 수 있을까요? 놀랍게도 백두산과 한라산 둘 다 휴화산이에요. 지각 아래에 여전히 마그마방이 존재하고 있기 때문이에요.

(A) Circle the best answer.

1. What is under the Earth's surface called?
   - ⓐ crust
   - ⓑ mantle
   - ⓒ volcanoes

2. What is magma made of?
   - ⓐ lava
   - ⓑ crust
   - ⓒ hot rocks

3. What happens when a volcano erupts?
   - ⓐ It becomes extinct.
   - ⓑ Lava erupts to the surface.
   - ⓒ The mantle becomes cold.
   - ⓓ The Earth's surface becomes two pieces.

4. What is NOT true about volcanoes?
   - ⓐ Active volcanoes produce lava.
   - ⓑ Extinct volcanoes are unable to erupt again.
   - ⓒ Some volcanoes won't erupt for a long time.
   - ⓓ Over 1,900 volcanoes will be extinct soon.

(B) Complete the sentences.

❶ .... erupt when magma under the crust comes out.

We call magma on the surface ❷ .... It only comes out of

❸ .... volcanoes.

Wrap Up   Fill in the blanks.

Volcanoes		
active volcanoes	❷ .... volcanoes	volcanoes not ❹ .... for a long time
magma erupts and becomes ❶	never erupt ❸	

lava   active   extinct   again

Science 8

Cave of Wonders!

R2_08.mp3

Caves are dark and mysterious. They are large, natural holes leading into Earth's surface. They are big enough for people and animals to enter and live. How were these large caves made? Most were formed by erosion. Erosion happens when the acid in water wears away rock. It can take millions of years for rock to erode. Son Doong in Vietnam is the largest cave in the world. It's over 2 million years old. It is much bigger than scientists first thought. It's about 9 kilometers long!

Read and Complete

1 Caves are large _____ leading into Earth's surface.

2 Caves are formed by _____.

Words to Know

- cave 동굴
- wonder 경이, 놀라움
- mysterious 불가사의한
- natural 자연적인
- hole 구멍
- enough 충분한, 충분히
- form 형성하다, 만들다
- erosion 부식, 침식
- acid 산(酸)
- wear away 닳게 만들다
- erode 부식하다, 침식하다
- Vietnam 베트남

배경지식 Plus!

세계에서 가장 깊은 동굴은 흑해 근처에 있는 크루베라(Krubera) 동굴이에요. 깊이가 무려 2,197미터랍니다. 세계에서 가장 큰 얼음동굴은 오스트리아에 있는 아이스리젠벨트(Eisriesenwelt) 동굴이에요. 원래 천연 석회동굴인데, 고도가 1,500미터나 되는 높은 지역에 있어서 동굴 속의 물이 얼면서 얼음동굴이 된 거예요.

A Circle the best answer.

1. What caused erosion?
   ⓐ acid in water   ⓑ rocks in water   ⓒ animals in caves

2. How long is the largest cave in the world?
   ⓐ about 2 kilometers long   ⓑ about 9 kilometers long
   ⓒ about 10 kilometers long

3. Why does the writer mention people and animals?
   ⓐ to explain how caves are formed
   ⓑ to emphasize how big some caves are
   ⓒ to give an example of a famous cave
   ⓓ to complain some caves were damaged

4. What is NOT true about Son Doong?
   ⓐ We can find it in Vietnam.
   ⓑ It's over 2 million years old.
   ⓒ It's the largest cave in the world.
   ⓓ It's much older than scientists first thought.

B Complete the sentences.

Caves are large holes in Earth's ❶_____. Erosion causes them.

❷_____ in water ❸_____ away rock over millions of years.

Wrap Up Fill in the blanks.

Caves		
의미	❶_____, natural ❷_____ leading into Earth's surface	acid
생성 방법	The ❸_____ in water wears away rocks.	erosion
	▶ ❹_____ happens over millions of years.	holes
가장 큰 동굴	Son Doong in Vietnam	large

From Birth to Death

R2_09.mp3

All living things on Earth have a life cycle. This cycle always includes birth and death. Each living thing has a unique cycle between being born and dying. For example, butterflies start as an egg. Then, the egg hatches and a larva is born. It eats and grows into a caterpillar. But it's still in the larva stage. Next, it builds a hard protective shell around itself. It's a pupa. After 10 to 14 days, an adult butterfly hatches from the shell. The butterfly then lays eggs before it dies, and the cycle begins again!

Read and Complete

❶ A butterfly starts its life cycle as an _____.

❷ A caterpillar builds a protective _____ and becomes a pupa.

Words to Know

□ **birth** 탄생, 출생
□ **living thing** 생물, 생명체
□ **life cycle** 생명 주기, 생애 주기
□ **include** 포함하다
□ **unique** 독특한, 고유의
□ **hatch** 부화하다
□ **larva** 유충
□ **caterpillar** 애벌레
□ **stage** 단계
□ **protective** 보호하는
□ **shell** 껍질
□ **pupa** 번데기
□ **lay** (알을) 낳다

배경지식 Plus!

독특한 **생애 주기(life cycle)**를 가진 대표적인 생물이 매미예요. 암컷 매미가 나무껍질에 알을 낳으면 그 알은 1년 후에 부화해요. 부화한 애벌레는 땅속으로 들어가 나무 뿌리의 즙을 먹으며 5년 정도 지내요. 그 후 땅 위로 올라와 껍질을 벗고 몸을 말린 후, 나무에 붙어 짝을 찾기 위해 크게 울어요.

A Circle the best answer.

1. What is the next step after an egg of a butterfly?
   ⓐ a pupa   ⓑ a larva   ⓒ an adult butterfly

2. What hatches from the protective shell?
   ⓐ an egg   ⓑ a caterpillar   ⓒ an adult butterfly

3. How does the life cycle of butterflies start again?
   ⓐ A butterfly eats as much food as it can.
   ⓑ A butterfly teaches its babies to get food.
   ⓒ A butterfly lays eggs before it dies.
   ⓓ A butterfly becomes a caterpillar again after it dies.

4. What is NOT true about the life cycle of butterflies?
   ⓐ A pupa has a hard protective shell.
   ⓑ A caterpillar is in the larva stage.
   ⓒ It starts with being born and ends with dying.
   ⓓ A caterpillar looks almost the same as an adult butterfly.

B Complete the sentences.

A life cycle begins with ❶........................ and ends with ❷........................ .

Different living things have ❸........................ life cycles between beginning

and end.

Wrap Up Fill in the blanks.

The Life Cycle of Butterflies

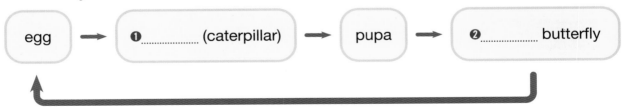

egg → ❶............ (caterpillar) → pupa → ❷............ butterfly

Science 10

Sources of Energy

R2_10.mp3

We use electricity for our computers and lights. That electricity is generated in power plants. Often, power plants use and burn non-renewable sources like coal, oil, or gas for energy. That's because they're easy to get and use. But most non-renewable sources generate air and water pollution. Also, they will run out someday. These days, scientists are improving renewable energy sources. Solar energy comes from the sun, so it's renewable. Wind power and hydrogen energy are also renewable energy sources. They produce almost no pollution and will never run out.

Read and Complete

❶ Power plants generate _____.

❷ Wind power is a _____ energy source.

Words to Know

- electricity 전기
- generate 발생시키다, 만들어 내다
- power plant 발전소
- non-renewable 재생이 안 되는
- source 원천, 자원
- coal 석탄
- pollution 오염, 공해
- run out 고갈되다
- improve 개선하다
- renewable 재생 가능한
- solar 태양의
- wind power 풍력
- hydrogen 수소
- produce 생산하다

배경지식 Plus!

우리가 버리는 쓰레기가 재생 에너지원이 될 수도 있어요. 폐기물을 변환시켜 에너지를 생산할 수 있거든요. 사업장이나 가정에서 발생되는 가연성 폐기물 중 에너지 함량이 높은 폐기물을 다양한 가공 처리 방법을 통해 고체 연료, 액체 연료, 가스 연료 등으로 생산하는 것이지요.

A Circle the best answer.

1. What is an example of a non-renewable source?

    ⓐ sun   ⓑ coal   ⓒ wind

2. Which energy source doesn't generate pollution?

    ⓐ oil   ⓑ gas   ⓒ hydrogen

3. Why do power plants often use non-renewable energy sources?

    ⓐ Because they are easy to use.
    ⓑ Because they will run out soon.
    ⓒ Because they generate air pollution.
    ⓓ Because they generate water pollution.

4. What is NOT true about renewable energy sources?

    ⓐ They will not run out.
    ⓑ They are made in plants.
    ⓒ They generate electricity.
    ⓓ They don't produce pollution.

B Complete the sentences.

Coal, oil, and gas are ❶_____ energy sources. They are easy to use but generate ❷_____. Renewable energy from the sun, wind, or ❸_____ are improving.

Wrap Up Fill in the blanks.

	non-renewable sources	renewable sources
예	• coal, oil, and gas	• ❸_____ and hydrogen energy, wind power
공해	• generate air and water ❶_____	• no pollution
특성	• easy to get and ❷_____ • run out someday	• ❹_____ run out

use   never   solar   pollution

Ⓐ Crossword Puzzle

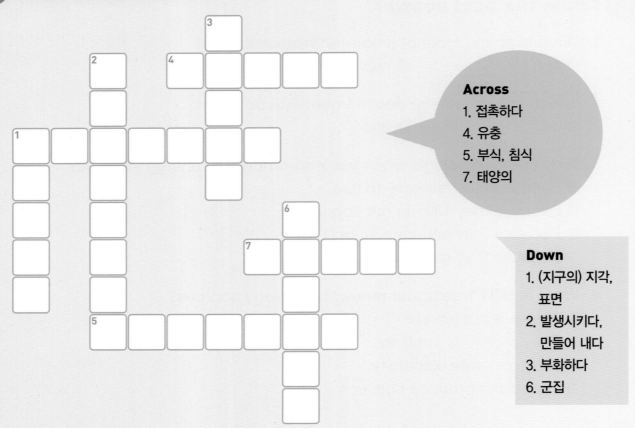

Across
1. 접촉하다
4. 유충
5. 부식, 침식
7. 태양의

Down
1. (지구의) 지각, 표면
2. 발생시키다, 만들어 내다
3. 부화하다
6. 군집

Ⓑ Match with the correct definition.

1. **cave** •

ⓐ Farmers use it on food crops to keep insects away.

2. **lava** •

ⓑ When magma comes to the surface, magma turns into it.

3. **pesticide** •

ⓒ a large, natural hole leading into Earth's surface

4. **pupa** •

ⓓ a butterfly in the stage between larva and adult

C Fill in the blanks with the correct words.

| erode | erupt | life cycle | non-renewable | pollution |

1. Lava can only _____ from active volcanoes.

용암은 활화산에서만 분출할 수 있습니다.

2. It can take millions of years for rock to _____.

암석이 부식하는 데는 수백만 년이 걸릴 수 있습니다.

3. The butterfly lays eggs before it dies, and the _____ begins again.

나비는 죽기 전에 알을 낳고, 다시 생애 주기가 시작됩니다.

4. Often, power plants burn _____ sources like coal or gas for energy.

보통, 발전소는 에너지를 얻기 위해 석탄과 가스 같은 재생이 안 되는 자원을 연소합니다.

5. Wind power and hydrogen energy produce almost no _____.

풍력과 수소 에너지는 오염을 거의 발생시키지 않습니다.

D Fill in the blanks with the correct expressions.

| hatches from | is made up of | get lost | run out | wears away |

1. Pesticides cause bees to _____ while looking for nectar.

2. The mantle _____ hot, red rocks.

3. Erosion happens when the acid in water _____ rock.

4. After 10 to 14 days, an adult butterfly _____ the shell.

5. Renewable energy sources will never _____.

Welcome to the Jungle

R2_11.mp3

We breathe in oxygen and breathe out carbon dioxide. Around 40% of Earth's oxygen comes from rainforests. You can find rainforests near the equator. The equator is a line. It goes around the middle of the Earth. Rainforests have a warm and wet environment. Plants grow well there. In rainforests, billions of plants produce oxygen and consume carbon dioxide. This helps keep oxygen and carbon dioxide in balance. This balance is important for plant and animal life on Earth. We can't breathe with too much or too little oxygen.

Read and Complete

① Rainforests produce a lot of _____.

② The _____ goes around the middle of the Earth.

Words to Know

- jungle 밀림(지대), 정글
- breathe 호흡하다
- oxygen 산소
- carbon dioxide 이산화탄소
- rainforest 열대 우림
- equator 적도
- the middle of ~의 가운데
- wet 습한, 축축한
- environment 환경
- billions of 수십억의 ~
- consume 소비하다
- balance 균형; 균형을 맞추다

배경지식 Plus!

아마존의 **열대 우림**(rainforest)은 전 세계 열대 우림의 40%를 차지하며, 지구에서 필요로 하는 산소의 4분의 1을 배출해요. 1960년대 이후 브라질에서는 개발 정책으로 아마존의 산림을 계속 파괴하고 있어요. 해마다 우리나라 면적의 5분에 4 정도가 사라지고 있다고 해요. 아마존 열대 우림은 기후 변화와 삼림 파괴로 인해 위기에 처해 있어요.

Comprehension Checkup

A Circle the best answer.

1. Where are most rainforests located?
ⓐ under the equator   ⓑ around the equator   ⓒ in the middle of the equator

2. What do plants consume?
ⓐ carbon dioxide   ⓑ oxygen   ⓒ oxygen and carbon dioxide

3. Why is the balance of oxygen and carbon dioxide important?
ⓐ Because plants can't grow with too much oxygen.
ⓑ Because people can't mix oxygen and carbon dioxide.
ⓒ Because people can't grow with too little carbon dioxide.
ⓓ Because people can't breathe if the balance is lost.

4. What is NOT true about rainforests?
ⓐ They have lots of plants.
ⓑ They are in warm and wet places.
ⓒ They produce 40% of Earth's carbon dioxide.
ⓓ They are important for life on Earth.

B Complete the sentences.

❶_____ are near the equator. They help the ❷_____

of carbon dioxide and oxygen in the air. This balance is important for life

on ❸_____.

Wrap Up Fill in the blanks.

Rainforests	
위치	near the ❶_____
기후	Warm and ❷_____ environment makes ❸_____ grow well.
환경적 역할	They keep oxygen and carbon dioxide in ❹_____.

balance

plants

equator

wet

37

Coyotes in the Arctic

R2_12.mp3

Coyotes are very adaptive to their environment. In North America, wolves and coyotes competed for food and territory. Wolves often killed people and farm animals. So, they were hunted to near extinction. This caused the coyote population to grow and expand in the last 200 years. They even expanded into northern Canada and Alaska. The harsh, cold environment forced the coyotes to adapt. Their fur color slowly changed to white. It let them hide better in the snow. Their fur also became thicker to protect them from the harsh cold.

Read and Complete

1 The coyote _____ began to grow as wolves disappeared.

2 Coyotes were forced to _____ in the cold environment.

Words to Know

□ coyote 코요테
□ adaptive 적응할 수 있는
□ North America
　 북아메리카 대륙, 북미
□ compete 경쟁하다
□ territory 영역
□ extinction 멸종
□ population 인구, 개체 수
□ expand 확장하다
□ Alaska 알래스카
□ harsh 혹독한
□ force 어쩔 수 없이 ~하게 만들다
□ adapt 적응하다

배경지식 Plus!

미국 원주민들 사이에서는 **코요테(coyote)**와 오소리의 특별한 친분이 유명하답니다. 코요테와 오소리는 먹이를 함께 잡는다고 해요. 주로 오소리가 땅속에서 설치류 등 소형 포유류의 굴을 파헤치고, 먹잇감이 땅 위로 모습을 드러내면 코요테가 잡는 방식으로 협력하는 것이지요. 이는 각자 사냥을 할 때보다 시간과 에너지 소모를 줄여 준다고 해요.

A Circle the best answer.

1. What did wolves and coyotes fight for?
 ⓐ areas to live ⓑ places with snow ⓒ people to live with

2. Where did the coyotes expand into?
 ⓐ Alaska ⓑ Europe ⓒ North America

3. Why did people hunt wolves?
 ⓐ Because wolves killed coyotes.
 ⓑ Because wolves killed farm animals.
 ⓒ Because wolves stole food from people.
 ⓓ Because people wanted to get their fur.

4. How did coyotes adapt to the harsh environment? (Choose 2 answers.)
 ⓐ Their fur got thicker to keep them warm.
 ⓑ They began to attack farms to find food.
 ⓒ They went north to expand their territory.
 ⓓ Their fur changed to a different color.

B Complete the sentences.

Coyotes and wolves competed, but people hunted ❶_____.

So, the coyote population grew quickly. Coyotes even ❷_____ into

the Alaska. They were able to ❸_____ to their new environment.

Wrap Up Number the sentences in order.

[3] The coyote population expanded into northern Canada and Alaska.

[ ] Wolves and coyotes competed for food and territory.

[ ] Coyotes adapted to the cold environment.

[ ] Wolves were hunted to near extinction.

Powerful Flash Floods

R2_13.mp3

Natural disasters can happen suddenly and unexpectedly. Flash floods are one type of disaster. A flash flood is when water levels rise within six hours of rainfall. Heavy rains or a broken dam raise the water level of rivers or streams. The rising water moves powerfully and quickly over land. It causes damage to property. And it can be deadly to people. In 2013, a flood in Kedarnath, India killed around 5,000 people! Local weather warnings can help you avoid these disasters. They can also tell you when to get to higher ground.

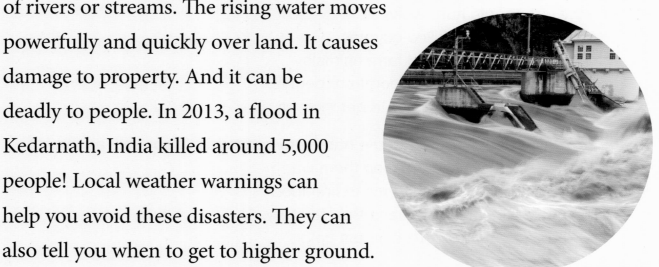

Read and Complete

1 Flash floods are a natural _____.

2 During a flash flood, water levels _____ suddenly.

Words to Know

- flash flood 갑작스러운 홍수
- natural disaster 자연 재해
- unexpectedly 뜻밖에, 갑자기
- water level 수위
- rise 오르다, 올라가다
- rainfall 강우
- heavy rain 폭우
- raise 올리다
- stream 시내
- damage 피해, 손해
- property 재산
- deadly 치명적인
- weather warning 기상 경보

배경피식 Plus!

2020년 1월, 인도네시아 자카르타 근처에서 기록적인 폭우로 인해 큰 홍수가 발생했어요. 그 지역의 40%가 물에 잠겼고, 약 40만 명의 사람들이 대피해야 했지요. 인도네시아 당국은 그 지역에서 불법적으로 만든 우물들이 지반을 약하게 하여 홍수에 취약했다고 발표했어요. 자연재해 역시 인간들의 욕심으로 더 심해지고 있는 걸까요?

(A) Circle the best answer.

1. **What is a sign of a flash flood?**
   ⓐ any rainfall   ⓑ high water levels   ⓒ property damage

2. **What can be helpful for people to avoid natural disasters?**
   ⓐ closing dams   ⓑ making long streams   ⓒ watching weather reports

3. **What is NOT true about flash floods?**
   ⓐ They destroy people's property.
   ⓑ Broken dams or heavy rain can cause floods.
   ⓒ We can prevent them in advance.
   ⓓ People should find higher ground when it happens.

4. **Why does the writer mention a flood in Kedarnath?**
   ⓐ to explain where flash floods happen often
   ⓑ to describe an example of a deadly flash flood
   ⓒ to emphasize the importance of weather warnings
   ⓓ to give an example of the most sudden flash flood

(B) Complete the sentences.

Natural disasters like ❶＿＿＿＿＿＿＿ floods can be deadly. During a

flash flood, ❷＿＿＿＿＿＿＿ levels rise unexpectedly. People should

watch weather ❸＿＿＿＿＿＿＿ when floods happen.

Wrap Up　Fill in the blanks.

Flash Floods		six
발생 조건	• water ❶＿＿＿ rise within ❷＿＿＿ hours of rainfall	dam
수위 상승의 원인	• heavy rains or a broken ❸＿＿＿	levels
결과	• cause ❹＿＿＿ to property • can be deadly to people	damage

Water and Iron

R2_14.mp3

Iron is a strong metal. People can shape it into useful things such as weapons and tools. People have used it for thousands of years. But, iron has a serious weakness. It can rust and decay, or break apart. Water and air cause a chemical reaction with iron. This reaction creates rust. Rust can make an iron tool useless. An iron tool outside in the rain will rust in a few days. To protect iron from rust, you can cover it with paint or oil.

Read and Complete

❶ People make lots of useful things with _____.

❷ Iron tools can be useless when they _____ and decay.

Words to Know

- iron 철, 쇠
- shape 형태를 만들다; 형태
- useful 유용한
- weapon 무기
- tool 도구, 연장
- serious 심각한
- weakness 약점
- rust 녹슬다; 녹
- decay 부식하다; 부식
- break apart 쪼개지다
- chemical 화학적인
- reaction 반응
- useless 쓸모 없는
- protect 보호하다

배경지식 Plus!

쇠(iron)로 만든 물건에 녹이 슬었을 때 녹을 쉽게 제거할 수 있는 방법이 있어요. 가장 손쉬운 방법은 녹슨 물건을 식초에 담그거나, 헝겊에 식초를 묻혀 녹슨 부분을 닦는 거예요. 녹슨 부분에 소금을 많이 뿌린 다음에 라임이나 레몬 껍질로 닦아 내는 것도 좋아요. 또는 베이킹 소다를 녹슨 부분에 많이 뿌린 후 물을 부어 잠시 둔 다음 닦아 냅니다.

A Circle the best answer.

1. What is the weakness of iron?
   - ⓐ rusting
   - ⓑ melting
   - ⓒ bending

2. A chemical reaction between what things makes rust?
   - ⓐ oil and iron
   - ⓑ water and air
   - ⓒ water and iron

3. How can you prevent iron from decaying?
   - ⓐ by painting it with oil
   - ⓑ by leaving it in the rain
   - ⓒ by placing it in a box
   - ⓓ by covering it with cardboard

4. What is NOT a feature of iron?
   - ⓐ It is a strong metal.
   - ⓑ It rusts as soon as it meets rain.
   - ⓒ It is a good material for weapons.
   - ⓓ It can be shaped into useful tools.

B Complete the sentences.

Iron is a strong metal and people ❶_____ it into weapons and

tools. Water and ❷_____ can cause it to rust. In order to

❸_____ iron from decay, it's good to cover it with paint or oil.

Wrap Up   Fill in the blanks.

Iron has a serious weakness.

원인	a chemical ❶_____ with ❷_____ and air
결과	It can ❸_____ and decay, or break apart.
보호 방법	You can ❹_____ it with paint or oil.

rust
cover
reaction
water

Endangered Polar Bears

R2_15.mp3

Humans are changing the environment. As our population grows and expands, we are destroying the habitats of several animals. Some animals fail to adapt to their changed habitats. Then, they become endangered. Polar bears are adapted to live in the Arctic. Their white fur keeps them warm and hidden. They are good at hunting seals and whales in Arctic waters. However, global warming is melting the Arctic ice. Polar bears' habitats are shrinking and disappearing. They cannot survive south of the Arctic. Soon, they may only live in zoos.

Read and Complete

① Humans are destroying animals' _____.

② Polar bears are one of the _____ animals.

Words to Know

- endangered 멸종 위기에 처한
- polar bear 북극곰
- destroy 파괴하다
- habitat 서식지
- the Arctic 북극
- hidden 숨은
- be good at ~에 능숙하다
- seal 바다표범, 물개
- whale 고래
- global warming 지구 온난화
- melt 녹다; 녹이다
- shrink 줄어들다, 감소하다

배경지식 Plus!

북극(the Arctic)의 얼음은 바닷물이 얼어서 만들어진 '해빙'으로 일반 얼음보다 2배 정도 빨리 녹는다고 해요. 최근 기온 상승으로 북극의 얼음이 사라지고 있어요. 그로 인해 바다사자들이 서식지를 이동하면서 먹이가 사라진 북극곰이 점점 더 북극에서 살아가기 힘들어지고 있는 것이죠.

A Circle the best answer.

1. What makes the Arctic ice melt?

ⓐ building zoos ⓑ global warming ⓒ endangered seals

2. What is happening to the polar bears' habitats?

ⓐ They're decreasing. ⓑ They're getting cold.
ⓒ Seals and whales are dying.

3. What is NOT an example of polar bears adapting to the Arctic?

ⓐ They can be in cold waters. ⓑ They hunt seals and whales.
ⓒ They can move to the south. ⓓ Their white fur helps them hide.

4. What can be inferred from the passage?

ⓐ Humans are the main factor of global warming.
ⓑ Humans are hunting polar bears to keep in zoos.
ⓒ South of the Arctic is too narrow for polar bears to live.
ⓓ Many people are visiting the Arctic to see polar bears.

B Complete the sentences.

Animal habitats are changing because of ❶............................... . Polar bears

live in the Arctic. But global warming is ❷............................... the Arctic ice.

Polar bears' habitats are shrinking and ❸............................... .

Wrap Up Fill in the blanks.

원인	• Humans change the ❶............................... . • We are destroying the habitats of ❷............................... .	animals habitats
결과	• Global ❸............................... is melting the Arctic ice. • Polar bears' ❹............................... are disappearing.	warming environment

WORD REVIEW

A Crossword Puzzle

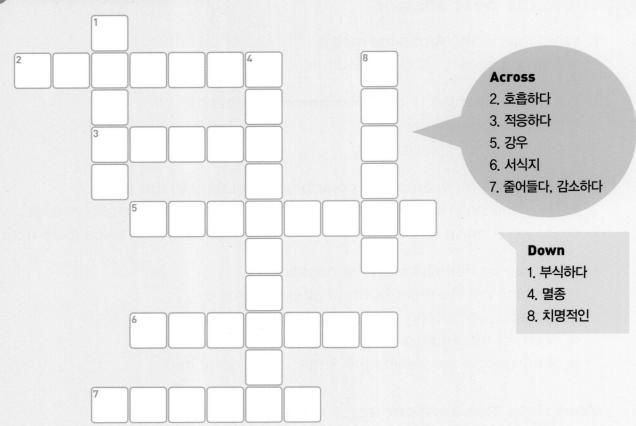

Across
2. 호흡하다
3. 적응하다
5. 강우
6. 서식지
7. 줄어들다, 감소하다

Down
1. 부식하다
4. 멸종
8. 치명적인

B Match with the correct definition.

1. endangered •

       ⓐ imaginary line around the middle of Earth

2. equator •

       ⓑ Floods and earthquakes are examples.

3. iron •

       ⓒ a strong metal

4. natural disaster •

       ⓓ When animals fail to adapt to their changed habitats, they become it.

Ⓒ Fill in the blanks with the correct words.

avoid	competed	consume	global warming	useless

1. Plants produce oxygen and _____ carbon dioxide.

식물들은 산소를 배출하고 이산화탄소를 소비합니다.

2. Wolves and coyotes _____ for food and territory.

늑대와 코요테는 먹이와 영역을 두고 경쟁했습니다.

3. Local weather warnings can help you _____ these disasters.

지역 기상 경보는 여러분이 이런 재해를 피할 수 있도록 도와줄 수 있습니다.

4. Rust can make an iron tool _____.

녹은 쇠 도구를 쓸모 없게 만들 수 있습니다.

5. _____ is melting the Arctic ice.

지구 온난화는 북극 얼음을 녹이고 있습니다.

Ⓓ Fill in the blanks with the correct expressions.

are good at	break apart	cause ~ to	forced ~ to	in balance

1. Rainforests keep oxygen and carbon dioxide _____.

2. The harsh environment _____ the coyotes _____ adapt.

3. Flash floods _____ damage _____ property.

4. Iron can rust and decay, or _____.

5. Polar bears _____ hunting seals and whales in Arctic waters.

Waves of Energy

R2_16.mp3

How can sunlight travel through space to Earth? It's because light is a type of electromagnetic wave(EW). EWs are energy, and they can travel through a vacuum. A vacuum is a place with no matter in it, like outer space. Radio waves are another type of EW. The waves can travel from your phone to a satellite in space. The satellite can then send those waves to someone on the other side of the world! Microwaves are also electromagnetic. They travel very fast, and they can cook food in minutes!

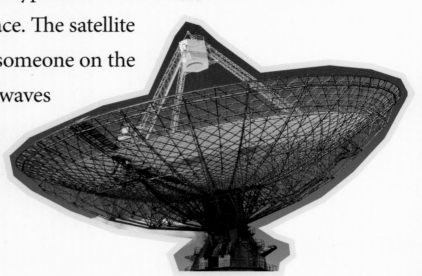

Read and Complete

1 A _____ is a place with no matter in it.

2 Electromagnetic waves _____ through space.

Words to Know

- **wave** 파동, 파장
- **travel** 이동하다
- **electromagnetic** 전자기의
- **vacuum** 진공
- **matter** 물질
- **outer space**
  우주 공간 (지구 대기권 밖의 공간)
- **radio wave** 전파
- **satellite** 위성
- **microwave**
  마이크로파, 극초단파
- **in minutes** 몇 분 안에

배경지식 Plus!

마이크로파(microwaves)를 이용하여 요리를 하는 제품이 바로 전자레인지입니다. '전자레인지'를 영어로 microwave oven이라고 해요. 마이크로파가 물질에 흡수되면서 분자를 진동시켜서 열을 내는 원리예요. 주로 수분이 많이 포함된 부분에 잘 흡수되어 그 부분이 먼저 뜨거워져요.

A Circle the best answer.

1. What is an example of a vacuum?

   ⓐ a satellite　　　ⓑ outer space　　　ⓒ electromagnetic waves

2. What is an example of an electromagnetic wave?

   ⓐ sound　　　ⓑ electricity　　　ⓒ sunlight

3. How do people use microwaves?

   ⓐ They use them to find their way.
   ⓑ They use them to cook food.
   ⓒ They use them to brighten the dark.
   ⓓ They use them to move around.

4. What does a satellite do with radio waves?

   ⓐ It helps radio waves to travel fast.
   ⓑ It makes radio waves much stronger.
   ⓒ It gathers various radio waves in the world.
   ⓓ It receives and sends radio waves from phones.

B Complete the sentences.

Electromagnetic waves like sunlight, ❶_____ waves, and

❷_____ can travel through a ❸_____. People use these

for many things, like talking to each other and cooking food.

Wrap Up　Fill in the blanks.

EW: ❶_____ wave		energy
특성	• waves of ❷_____ • travel through a ❸_____	electromagnetic microwaves
종류	• sunlight, radio waves, ❹_____	vacuum

49

The Journey of the Moon

R2_17.mp3

Every night, the moon looks a little different. That's because each night it is at a different stage of its journey. The moon travels around the Earth in 29.53 days. Each month, the moon goes through 8 phases. The first phase is the new moon. New moons appear very small because they reflect little of the sun's light. It eventually grows into a full moon. It reflects the sun's light like a circle. Over the next phases, the moon appears smaller and smaller. Then, it returns to a new moon.

Read and Complete

❶ The moon moves around the _____.

❷ The moon has 8 phases according to its _____.

Words to Know

- □ journey 여정, 이동
- □ a little 약간
- □ go through (일련의 과정이나 절차를) 거치다
- □ phase (주기적으로 형태가 변하는 달의) 위상, 모습
- □ new moon 초승달
- □ appear 나타나다, 보이기 시작하다
- □ reflect 반사하다
- □ little 거의 없는
- □ eventually 결국
- □ full moon 보름달
- □ return 되돌아가다

배경지식 Plus!

달이 지구를 공전하는 29.53일 동안 달의 형태가 변하는 것을 '달의 위상 변화'라고 해요. 달의 위상 (phase)은 '삭 → 초승달 → 상현달 → 상현망 → 망(보름달) → 하현망 → 하현달 → 그믐달 → 삭'의 순서로 변합니다. 달은 스스로 빛을 내지 못하고 햇빛을 받는 부분만 빛을 반사하여 밝게 보이므로, 태양과 지구, 달의 위치에 따라 지구에서 보이는 모습이 달라져요.

(A) Circle the best answer.

1. **How long does it take for the moon to travel around the Earth?**
   ⓐ 8 days   ⓑ 29.53 days   ⓒ 8 months

2. **What makes the moon appear bigger and smaller?**
   ⓐ the sunlight it reflects   ⓑ its speed when traveling
   ⓒ its distance from the Earth

3. **Why does the moon look different every night?**
   ⓐ Because it regularly appears and disappears.
   ⓑ Because sometimes it fails to reflect sun's light.
   ⓒ Because it shows us a different phase as it travels.
   ⓓ Because the weather is different from night to night.

4. **What is NOT true about the moon?**
   ⓐ People call the first phase the new moon.
   ⓑ A new moon becomes smaller to a full moon.
   ⓒ A full moon reflects the sun's light like a circle.
   ⓓ A new moon doesn't reflect much of the sun's light.

(B) Complete the sentences.

The moon goes through 8 ❶_____ as it travels. At each phase, it ❷_____

more or less sunlight. This makes the moon look bigger or ❸_____.

Wrap Up   Fill in the blanks.

The moon ❶_____ around the Earth.		circle
a ❷_____ moon	small, reflect little of the sun's ❸_____	travels
		light
a full moon	reflect the sun's light like a ❹_____	new

51

Roles in the Food Chain

R2_18.mp3

Plants and animals live in a habitat. All habitats have a food chain. Food chains are made up of producers, consumers, and decomposers. Let's take a look at an example in a habitat like the African plains. Plants and grass produce energy from the sun and the ground. These producers are then eaten by a consumer, such as a zebra. The zebra uses the plant's energy to grow. When the zebra dies, it falls to the ground. Decomposers, such as worms and bacteria, turn the zebra's energy into the soil. Producers then use that energy to make food!

Read and Complete

1 Producers, consumers, and _____ live together in a habitat.

2 Consumers eat _____.

Words to Know

- food chain 먹이 사슬
- be made up of
  ~으로 구성되다
- producer 생산자
- consumer 소비자
- decomposer 분해자
- take a look at ~을 살펴보다
- plain 평원, 초원
- produce 생산하다
- ground 땅
- worm 지렁이
- bacteria 박테리아
- soil 흙

배경피식 Plus!

먹이 사슬(food chain)은 생산자, 소비자, 분해자로 구성되지만, 실제로는 좀더 복잡해요. 사슴이 풀을 뜯어 먹고 호랑이가 그 사슴을 잡아먹으면, 사슴이 1차 소비자이고 호랑이가 2차 소비자가 됩니다. 이렇게 실제 생태계에서는 여러 먹이 사슬이 복잡하게 얽혀 있는데, 그것을 '먹이 그물'이라고 해요.

(A) Circle the best answer.

1. How do plants get energy?
ⓐ from the consumers   ⓑ from the animals   ⓒ from the sun and soil

2. What is an example of a decomposer?
ⓐ grass   ⓑ worm   ⓒ zebra

3. What do decomposers do?
ⓐ They eat producers.
ⓑ They kill consumers, such as zebras.
ⓒ They produce energy from plants.
ⓓ They return energy to the ground.

4. What is NOT true about food chains?
ⓐ They are found in habitats.
ⓑ Producers are eaten by consumers.
ⓒ Consumers are the most important.
ⓓ Decomposers break down consumers.

(B) Complete the sentences.

Each ❶_____ has a food chain. Food chains are made up of

producers, consumers, and decomposers. ❷_____ get energy from

producers. They return it to the ❸_____ by decomposers.

Wrap Up   Connect.

Food Chain

❶ Producers   •   • ⓐ turn the consumers' energy into the soil.

❷ Consumers   •   • ⓑ produce energy from the sun and ground.

❸ Decomposers   •   • ⓒ eat producers.

Science 19

Four Important Spheres

R2_19.mp3

The Earth consists of four systems. We call them spheres. The first system is the biosphere. It includes all living things on Earth. Next, the geosphere system is all of the rocks and minerals on Earth. All of the water on Earth is part of the hydrosphere. Finally, the atmosphere is the gases or air, and it surrounds Earth. These 4 systems are all closely connected. For example, wind from the atmosphere causes erosion in the geosphere. All the plants and animals of the biosphere need water from the hydrosphere.

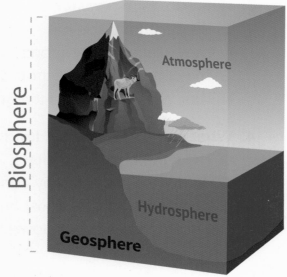

Atmosphere

Biosphere

Hydrosphere

Geosphere

Read and Complete

❶ The Earth has four systems called _____.

❷ The four systems are _____ closely.

Words to Know

- □ **sphere** 영역, ~권
- □ **consist of** ~으로 구성되다
- □ **system** 시스템, 체계
- □ **biosphere** 생물권
- □ **include** 포함하다
- □ **geosphere** 지권
- □ **mineral** 광물
- □ **hydrosphere** 수권
- □ **atmosphere** 대기권
- □ **surround** 둘러싸다
- □ **closely** 밀접하게
- □ **connect** 연결하다

배경지식 Plus!

지구의 네 개의 **권역(sphere)** 안에서 아주 다양한 생물학적, 물리학적 과정들이 서로 긴밀하게 영향을 주고받으며 일어나고 있어요. 네 권역 이름을 쉽게 풀어 볼게요. '권역'을 뜻하는 sphere 앞 글자만 살펴볼까요? bio-는 그리스어로 '생명'을 의미하고, geo-는 '땅', hydro-는 '물', atmo-는 '공기'를 의미해요. 어려운 이름들이 이제는 쉽게 다가오지요?

A Circle the best answer.

1. **Which system are humans in?**
   - ⓐ biosphere
   - ⓑ hydrosphere
   - ⓒ atmosphere

2. **What is a part of the geosphere?**
   - ⓐ rain
   - ⓑ minerals
   - ⓒ plants

3. **How does the atmosphere affect the geosphere?**
   - ⓐ Animals eat plants.
   - ⓑ Heavy rain causes floods.
   - ⓒ Plants need water to grow.
   - ⓓ Wind slowly causes erosion of rocks and soil.

4. **What can be an example of the connection between the biosphere and the atmosphere?**
   - ⓐ People pollute the air.
   - ⓑ People eat other animals.
   - ⓒ People live on the ground.
   - ⓓ People dig valuable minerals.

B Complete the sentences.

The Earth's four systems include the ❶_____, atmosphere,

geosphere, and ❷_____. These spheres are all

❸_____ connected.

Wrap Up Fill in the blanks.

Earth's Systems

biosphere	geosphere	hydrosphere	atmosphere
all ❶_____ things	rocks and ❷_____	❸_____	gases or air surrounding ❹_____

minerals   living   water   Earth

Twinkle, Twinkle, Little Star

R2_20.mp3

Why do some stars in the sky look brighter than others? The apparent magnitude of a star is how bright it looks to us. We measure it with the brightness of the star and its distance from Earth. The sun appears really bright. That's because it's very large and close to Earth. However, the absolute magnitude is how bright a star really is. Many stars far away in space are bigger and brighter than the sun. But they appear less bright than the sun. They have a greater absolute magnitude than their apparent magnitude.

Read and Complete

① The _____ magnitude tells us how bright a star looks.

② The _____ magnitude is how bright a star really is.

Words to Know

- twinkle 반짝거리다; 반짝거림
- apparent magnitude
  시등급(지구에서 보이는 별의 밝기)
- measure 측정하다, 재다
- brightness 밝기
- distance 거리
- absolute magnitude
  절대등급(별의 실제 밝기)
- far away 멀리 떨어진

배경지식 Plus!

태양보다 절대등급(absolute magnitude)이 높은 별은 약 83개예요. 현재까지 관측된 별 중 가장 밝은 것은 태양의 절대등급의 870만 배로 빛난다고 해요. 시등급(apparent magnitude)은 '겉보기 등급'이라고 하며, 눈으로 보았을 때 가장 어두운 6등급 별은 가장 밝은 1등급 별보다 100배 어두워요.

A Circle the best answer.

1. **What do people NOT use to measure apparent magnitude?**
   ⓐ the brightness of the star   ⓑ the number of nearby stars
   ⓒ the distance of the star from Earth

2. **What do people consider to measure absolute magnitude?**
   ⓐ the brightness of the star itself   ⓑ the distance of the star from Earth
   ⓒ the distance of the star from the sun

3. **Why does the sun appear really bright?**
   ⓐ Because it's far away from Earth.
   ⓑ Because it's the brightest star in space.
   ⓒ Because it's very big and close to Earth.
   ⓓ Because it doesn't have any stars around it.

4. **Why do some big and bright stars look less bright to us?**
   ⓐ Because they're far away from Earth.
   ⓑ Because they often cover each other.
   ⓒ Because their temperatures are too high.
   ⓓ Because they're too close to the sun.

B Complete the sentences.

Apparent magnitude is how bright a star appears from ❶_____.

The absolute magnitude tells us how bright a star ❷_____ is.

Wrap Up   Fill in the blanks.

apparent magnitude	❶_____ magnitude	
• how bright a star looks from Earth		absolute
▸ the ❷_____ of a star	• how bright a star	brightness
▸ a star's ❸_____ from Earth	❹_____ is	really
		distance

A Crossword Puzzle

Across
2. (달의) 위상, 모습
3. 나타나다, 보이기 시작하다
6. 연결하다
8. 광물

Down
1. 물질
4. 박테리아
5. 되돌아가다
7. 평원, 초원

B Match with the correct definition.

1. decomposer • ⓐ a place with no matter in it

2. new moon • ⓑ a first phase of the moon's journey

3. soil • ⓒ part of the food chain that breaks down consumers

4. vacuum • ⓓ the substance on the surface of the earth in which plants grow

C **Fill in the blanks with the correct words.**

| includes | measure | reflects | satellite | surrounds |

1. Radio waves can travel from your phone to a _____ in space.
전파는 여러분의 전화기에서 우주 내의 위성으로 이동할 수 있습니다.

2. A full moon _____ the sun's light like a circle.
보름달은 태양의 빛을 원처럼 반사합니다.

3. The atmosphere is the gases or air, and it _____ Earth.
대기권은 가스나 공기이고, 지구를 둘러싸고 있습니다.

4. The biosphere _____ all living things on Earth.
생물권은 지구상의 모든 생명체를 포함합니다.

5. We _____ the apparent magnitude with the brightness of the star and its distance from Earth.
우리는 시등급을 별의 밝기와 지구로부터의 거리로 측정합니다.

D **Fill in the blanks with the correct expressions.**

| consists of | far away | in minutes | goes through | take a look at |

1. Microwaves travel so fast, and they can cook food _____.

2. Each month, the moon _____ 8 phases.

3. Let's _____ an example in a habitat like the African plains.

4. The Earth _____ four systems, and we call them spheres.

5. Many stars _____ in space are bigger and brighter than the sun.

R2_21.mp3

Neighborhoods vs. Communities

When the teacher was explaining something, I was confused. So I put up my hand. "What's the difference between a neighborhood and a community? I don't get it." He answered, "A neighborhood is where you and your neighbors live. It's a physical place, and you can find it on a map. My neighborhood is in South Chicago. On the other hand, a community is a group of people, and they have something in common such as race, occupation, or interests. In my neighborhood, for example, we have a large Asian community and a community of volunteers."

Read and Complete

1 The teacher explains a _____ and a community.

2 The people in a community have something in _____.

Words to Know

- **neighborhood**
  (특정) 지역, 지방
- **community** 공동체, 지역 사회
- **confused**
  혼란스러운, 헷갈리는
- **put up** 올리다, 들다
- **difference** 차이
- **neighbor** 이웃 사람
- **physical** 물리적인
- **on the other hand** 반면에
- **have something in common** 공통점이 있다
- **race** 인종
- **occupation** 직업
- **Asian** 아시아인
- **volunteer** 자원봉사자

배경지식 Plus!

공동체(community)는 지역과 공간에 얽매이지 않고 공통의 가치로 만들어지는 것이 특징이에요. 특히 요즘에는 인터넷 기술을 기반으로 하여 SNS, 홈페이지, 블로그, 카페 등 사이버 커뮤니티가 활발하게 조직되고 운영되고 있어요. 사이버 커뮤니티가 오프라인 커뮤니티로 발전하여 새로운 역할을 하기도 한답니다.

Comprehension Checkup

(A) Circle the best answer.

1. Where is the teacher's neighborhood?

ⓐ Asia   ⓑ community   ⓒ South Chicago

2. What is NOT a community?

ⓐ an area of New York   ⓑ a group of Koreans in LA.

ⓒ a group of lawyers in New York

3. What is a neighborhood?

ⓐ It's a map of a city or a town.   ⓑ It's a place where people live.

ⓒ It's a special place for the same race.

ⓓ It has something in common with jobs.

4. Why does the teacher mention a community of volunteers?

ⓐ to give an example of a neighborhood

ⓑ to indicate his neighborhood on the map

ⓒ to say that he is interested in volunteering

ⓓ to compare a neighborhood and a community

(B) Complete the sentences.

A neighborhood is where your ❶_____ live. You can find it on a

❷_____. A ❸_____ is a group of people. They have

something in common such as jobs and hobbies.

Wrap Up   Fill in the blanks.

neighborhood	community	
❶_____ places	• a group of ❸_____ with	race
• where neighbors	things in common	live
❷_____	• ❹_____, occupation,	physical
	interest	people

Merry Kwanzaa!

R2_22.mp3

Most African Americans wake up early on December 26. It's the first day of Kwanzaa. Kwanzaa is an African American holiday. It connects African Americans to their traditional African culture. They celebrate their African identity. African families in America put up African flags. And they prepare a large feast. They have the feast together with family and friends. Then, they play traditional African drums. Everyone dances to the rhythm. January 1 is the last day of Kwanzaa. Time to open the Kwanzaa presents!

Read and Complete

1 African American families hold a big _____ with their friends.

2 People dance to the _____ of African drums.

Words to Know

- **African American** 아프리카계 미국인
- **holiday** 휴일, 명절
- **connect A to B** A를 B에 연결하다
- **traditional** 전통적인
- **celebrate** 기념하다
- **identity** 정체성
- **flag** 깃발
- **prepare** 준비하다
- **feast** 연회, 잔치
- **rhythm** 리듬

배경지식 Plus!

콴자(Kwanzaa)는 '첫 추수'라는 의미로, 아프리카계 미국인들에게는 중요한 축제예요. 요즘에는 크리스마스와 함께 콴자를 즐기는 가정들이 많아서, 크리스마스 장식과 함께 콴자의 상징인 '키나라'라는 7개의 촛대 장식을 해요. 각 초는 '단합, 자결, 협동과 책임, 협력, 목적, 창의, 신념'을 나타낸다고 해요.

Comprehension Checkup

A Circle the best answer.

1. Who celebrates Kwanzaa?
   - ⓐ Africans
   - ⓑ Americans in Africa
   - ⓒ African Americans

2. When do they open the presents?
   - ⓐ after Kwanzaa is finished
   - ⓑ on the last day of Kwanzaa
   - ⓒ on the first day of Kwanzaa

3. Why is Kwanzaa meaningful to African Americans?
   - ⓐ Because it allows them to go back to Africa.
   - ⓑ Because it shows the power of African music.
   - ⓒ Because it introduces African culture to Americans.
   - ⓓ Because it links them to their traditional African culture.

4. What is NOT true about Kwanzaa?
   - ⓐ People hang African flags.
   - ⓑ People enjoy it for 3 or 4 days.
   - ⓒ People prepare a gift for each other.
   - ⓓ People eat and dance at the parties.

B Complete the sentences.

Kwanzaa is a big holiday for African ❶............................ . Kwanzaa lets them enjoy their ❷............................ culture. They celebrate their African ❸............................ .

Wrap Up Fill in the blanks.

기간, 의미	from December 26 to January 1, ❶............................ American holiday	celebrate
기념하는 것	African Americans ❷............................ their traditional culture.	African
이유	They are proud of their African ❸............................ .	feast
하는 일	They have a large ❹............................ together.	identity

What You Can Buy

R2_23.mp3

What do you usually buy with your money? Money can be used to buy goods or services. Goods are physical things, so you can see or touch them. A meal from a restaurant is a good. It takes money to make goods, so it costs money to buy them. Services are what people do to earn money. Servers in a restaurant provide a service by bringing the meals to customers. Their time, skill, and effort cost money. Customers pay for both goods and services at places like stores and restaurants.

Read and Complete

❶ People use money to buy _____ and services.

❷ _____ at restaurants pay for services.

Words to Know

- □ **goods** 상품
- □ **service** 서비스
- □ **physical** 물질의, 실체가 있는
- □ **meal** 식사
- □ **cost** (비용이) ~이다/들다
- □ **earn** (돈을) 벌다
- □ **provide** 제공하다
- □ **customer** 고객
- □ **skill** 기술
- □ **effort** 노력
- □ **pay** (비용을) 지불하다

배경지식 Plus!

상품(**goods**)과 서비스(**service**)는 또 어떤 차이가 있을까요? 상품의 질은 평가하기가 간단하고 쉽지만 서비스의 질을 평가하는 것은 상대적이고 복잡해요. 상품은 보관할 수 있지만 서비스는 보관이 불가능해요. 또한 상품은 생산되고 나서 소비되기까지 시간이 필요하지만, 서비스는 제공되는 동시에 소비가 됩니다.

Comprehension Checkup

A Circle the best answer.

1. **What is an example of goods?**
   ⓐ concerts   ⓑ hamburgers   ⓒ bus rides

2. **What is an example of a service?**
   ⓐ a book   ⓑ a phone   ⓒ a piano lesson

3. **What is true about goods?**
   ⓐ You can't see or touch goods.
   ⓑ People like customers can be goods.
   ⓒ Money is needed to make goods.
   ⓓ Goods are time and skill for you.

4. **Why should customers pay for services?**
   ⓐ Because effort to provide services costs money.
   ⓑ Because services are actions to make food.
   ⓒ Because services are free for the customers.
   ⓓ Because services are provided by customers.

B Complete the sentences.

Customers use ❶_____ for goods and services. Goods are

❷_____ things. Services are what people do to ❸_____

money.

Wrap Up Fill in the blanks.

Customers pay ❶_____ for…		goods
❷_____	❸_____	time
• physical things	• people's actions	services
• You can see or touch them.	• ❹_____, skill, effort	money

65

R2_24.mp3

Remembering Heroes

Soldiers keep their countries safe. Sometimes, they take part in a war, and even give their lives to protect their countries. Memorial Day in America is a holiday dedicated to fallen soldiers. It was started in 1868 after the American Civil War. American citizens remember their soldiers' sacrifice on Memorial Day. They visit cemeteries and bring flowers. Many volunteers place American flags on soldiers' graves. Memorial Day is on the last Monday of May. Most workers and students have the day off. It is important not to forget the noble sacrifice soldiers made.

Read and Complete

1 Some soldiers died to _____ their countries.

2 Sometimes, soldiers fight in a _____.

Words to Know

- hero 영웅
- soldier 군인
- take part in ~에 참여하다
- Memorial Day 현충일
- dedicated 바치는, 헌정하는
- fallen 전사한, 쓰러진
- Civil War 미국 남북 전쟁
- citizen 시민
- sacrifice 희생
- cemetery 묘지
- grave 무덤
- day off 휴일
- noble 숭고한

배경지식 Plus!

나라마다 나라를 위해 목숨 바친 군인들을 기리는 국경일이 있어요. 우리나라에는 현충일(6월 6일)이 있지요. 6·25 전쟁의 참전용사들을 비롯한 선열들의 넋을 기리는 날로, 1956년에 처음 지정되었어요. 영국에는 Remembrance Day라는 국경일이 있어요. 제1차 세계대전의 휴전기념일인 11월 11일의 바로 앞 일요일에 해당해요.

A Circle the best answer.

1. What does Memorial Day celebrate?
   ⓐ hard workers   ⓑ brave citizens   ⓒ fallen soldiers

2. When was Memorial Day started?
   ⓐ after the American Civil War   ⓑ after the last Monday of May
   ⓒ after many volunteers' day off

3. Why is Memorial Day important?
   ⓐ Because it keeps America safe.
   ⓑ Because it gives volunteers more work to do.
   ⓒ Because it lets people remember soldiers' sacrifice.
   ⓓ Because it is one of the biggest American holidays.

4. What do American citizens NOT do on Memorial Day?
   ⓐ They remember fallen soldiers.   ⓑ They experience a war.
   ⓒ They put flags on graves.   ⓓ They bring flowers to cemeteries.

B Complete the sentences.

Memorial Day is dedicated to fallen soldiers. American citizens

❶_____ the soldiers' sacrifice to protect their country. They bring

❷_____ and flags to the soldiers' ❸_____.

Wrap Up   Fill in the blanks.

Memorial Day		
날짜	• the last ❶_____ of May	
의미	• a holiday to ❷_____ fallen soldiers	
하는 일	• remember soldiers' ❸_____	
	• visit ❹_____ with flowers and flags	

cemeteries

remember

sacrifice

Monday

R2_25.mp3

A Good Source of Information

Julius Caesar is in many history museums and books. He lived over 2,000 years ago. He was a Roman politician. We know about his life from primary sources. Primary sources are letters and pictures from the past. Caesar kept a journal, and it survived until modern times. Historians learned a lot about his life from his journal. We can also see Caesar's appearance on ancient Roman coins. These primary sources help us understand people from the past. Without them, much of their past would be a mystery.

Read and Complete

1 Julius Caesar was a _____ of Rome.

2 Historians studied _____ sources to know Caesar's life.

Words to Know

- **Roman** 고대 로마의
- **politician** 정치가
- **primary** 최초의, 주요한
- **primary source** 1차 자료
- **past** 과거
- **journal** 일기
- **modern times** 현대
- **historian** 역사학자
- **appearance** 외모
- **ancient** 고대의
- **coin** 동전
- **mystery** 미스터리, 수수께끼

배경지식 Plus!

영어 단어 Caesar(시저)는 황제 중에서도 실권을 장악하고 권력을 마음대로 휘두르는 전제군주나 독재자에게 붙이는 호칭이에요. Caesar라는 단어는 로마의 정치가였던 율리우스 카이사르(Julius Caesar)로부터 비롯되었어요. Caesar(카이사르)라는 이름이 영어식으로 '시저'라고 발음된 것이지요.

Comprehension Checkup

A Circle the best answer.

1. Which primary source did Caesar make?
ⓐ a journal　　ⓑ a museum　　ⓒ a historian

2. How do we know what Caesar looked like?
ⓐ from coins　　ⓑ from letters　　ⓒ from books

3. What is NOT a primary source?
ⓐ coins　　　　　　　　ⓑ letters
ⓒ museums　　　　　　ⓓ journals

4. Why are primary sources important?
ⓐ Because they lived over 2,000 years.
ⓑ Because they make the past mysterious.
ⓒ Because they make historians study Rome.
ⓓ Because they help us know historical people.

B Complete the sentences.

❶_____ use primary sources to understand the past. Roman coins showed us what Julius Caesar ❷_____ like. His ❸_____ told us about his life.

Wrap Up　Fill in the blanks.

Primary Sources

종류	letters and pictures from the ❶_____
의미	help us ❷_____ people from the past
예시	Julius Caesar's ❸_____: ❹_____ learned a lot about his life.

understand

journal

historians

past

69

WORD REVIEW

A Crossword Puzzle

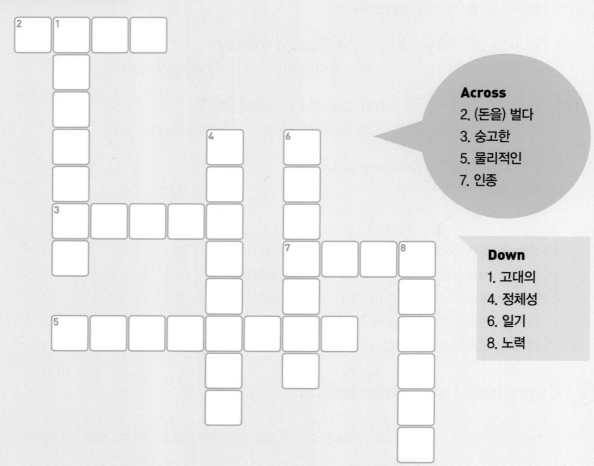

Across
2. (돈을) 벌다
3. 숭고한
5. 물리적인
7. 인종

Down
1. 고대의
4. 정체성
6. 일기
8. 노력

B Match with the correct definition.

1. community •

   ⓐ where you and your neighbors live

2. goods •

   ⓑ a group of people with something in common

3. neighborhood •

   ⓒ physical things that you can see or touch

4. primary sources •

   ⓓ letters and pictures from the past

C Fill in the blanks with the correct words.

dedicated	mystery	prepare	provide	sacrifice

1. African Americans _____ a large feast to celebrate Kwanzaa.

아프리카계 미국인들은 콴자를 기념하기 위해 큰 잔치를 준비합니다.

2. Servers _____ a service by bringing the meals to customers.

종업원들은 고객들에게 식사를 가져다줌으로써 서비스를 제공합니다.

3. Memorial Day is a holiday _____ to fallen soldiers.

현충일은 전사한 군인들에게 헌정하는 공휴일입니다.

4. It is important not to forget the noble _____ soldiers made.

군인들이 했던 숭고한 희생을 잊지 않는 것이 중요합니다.

5. Without primary sources, much of the past would be a _____.

1차 자료가 없으면, 과거의 많은 부분이 수수께끼일 것입니다.

D Fill in the blanks with the correct expressions.

connects ~ to	pay for	for example	put up	take part in

1. When the teacher was explaining something, I was confused and _____ my hand.

2. Kwanzaa _____ African Americans _____ their traditional African culture.

3. In my neighborhood, _____, we have a large Asian community.

4. Customers _____ both goods and services at places like restaurants.

5. Sometimes, soldiers _____ a war.

Social Studies
26

Money and Interest

R2_26.mp3

Where do you keep your money? Most kids have a piggy bank or another safe place to keep their money. Most adults use regular banks. Banks keep peoples' money safe and pay interest for it. Interest is the cost of money. So, you can make money by saving it in a bank. Meanwhile, banks use customers' saved money. They lend it to other people. The borrowers must pay back the money on time and pay interest for it to the bank. In this way, interest lets both people and banks earn some money.

Read and Complete

❶ People keep their _____ in a bank.

❷ Banks pay _____ for customers' money.

Words to Know
- **interest** 이자
- **piggy bank** 돼지 저금통
- **adult** 성인, 어른
- **regular** 보통의, 자주 다니는
- **keep A safe** A를 안전하게 보관하다
- **meanwhile** 한편
- **lend** 빌려주다
- **borrower** 빌린 사람, 대출자
- **on time** 시간을 어기지 않고
- **earn** (돈을) 벌다

배경지식 Plus!
'예금'과 '적금'의 차이를 알고 있나요? 정기 예금이란 목돈을 일정기간 은행에 보관해 두는 거예요. 만기가 되면 보관해 둔 원금과 그에 대한 **이자(interest)**를 함께 받아요. 적금은 매월 일정 금액을 저축하는 거예요. 보통 적금보다 예금의 이율이 높은 편인데, 은행이 고객이 맡겨 둔 목돈을 운용하여 수입을 올리기 쉽기 때문이지요.

Comprehension Checkup

(A) Circle the best answer.

1. Where do people NOT keep their money?
   ⓐ safe places   ⓑ piggy banks   ⓒ regular places

2. What is the cost of money?
   ⓐ safety   ⓑ interest   ⓒ borrower

3. How can you make money by using a bank?
   ⓐ Banks keep your money and give you interest.
   ⓑ You can keep your money safe with no interest.
   ⓒ You can lend your money to banks with interest.
   ⓓ You can get interest by introducing banks to your friends.

4. How do banks make money?
   ⓐ Borrowers pay interest to banks.
   ⓑ Banks connect lenders and borrowers.
   ⓒ Banks keep the customers' saved money.
   ⓓ Customers pay interest to banks for saving their money.

(B) Complete the sentences.

People ❶_____ their money in banks. Banks give them some interest.

Banks use customers' saved money to ❷_____ it to other people.

Borrowers should ❸_____ back the money with some interest.

Wrap Up   Fill in the blanks.

Who	What They Do	About Interest
customer	❶_____ their money safe in banks	❷_____ interest
bank	They ❸_____ customers' money to other people.	Borrowers ❹_____ back with interest.

pay   lend   keep   get

Laws and Rules

R2_27.mp3

Parents and teachers make rules to keep children safe. The government also makes rules to keep citizens safe. It's one of the many functions of a government. Politicians make laws for citizens to follow. They can make laws against killing and stealing, for example. Those are universal laws. Every country has these laws. However, governments often make local laws. These laws are important to the residents in that area. In Singapore, for example, it's against the law to feed pigeons. But in most other countries, you can!

Read and Complete

❶ Laws help keep _____ safe.

❷ Governments make both _____ and local laws.

Words to Know

- □ **law** 법
- □ **rule** 규칙
- □ **government** 정부
- □ **function** 기능
- □ **politician** 정치인
- □ **against** ～에 반대하여
- □ **steal** 훔치다
- □ **universal** 보편적인
- □ **local** 지역의, 현지의
- □ **resident** 주민
- □ **Singapore** 싱가포르
- □ **pigeon** 비둘기

배경지식 Plus!

미국의 특이한 지역 법을 알아봐요. 인디애놀라에서는 아이스크림 트럭이 불법이라고 해요. 시내에 푸드 트럭 형태의 상점들이 많아지는 것을 방지하기 위해서예요. 마운트버논에서는 공원에서 꽃을 꺾는 것이 불법이에요. 또한 밤 10시 30분 이후에는 소프트볼장에 소등이 되며 소프트볼을 하는 것이 법으로 금지되어 있기도 해요.

Comprehension Checkup

(A) Circle the best answer.

1. What is one thing that universal laws want to prevent?

ⓐ smoking   ⓑ raising pigeons   ⓒ stealing something

2. What is one thing that local laws want to prevent?

ⓐ following rules   ⓑ feeding pigeons   ⓒ killing someone

3. What is NOT true about laws?

ⓐ Politicians make laws.

ⓑ Citizens should follow laws.

ⓒ Local laws are the same everywhere.

ⓓ Laws against killing people are universal.

4. What can be inferred about politicians from the passage?

ⓐ They don't have to follow laws.

ⓑ They can make local laws only.

ⓒ They have to live in a certain area.

ⓓ They work for governments and citizens.

(B) Complete the sentences.

Politicians in a government make ❶_____ to keep its citizens safe.

❷_____ laws must be followed everywhere, but ❸_____

laws are only for certain places.

Wrap Up   Fill in the blanks.

Making Laws		country
목적	• to keep citizens ❶_____	safe
종류	• ❷_____ laws: for every ❸_____ • local laws: for residents in that ❹_____	universal area

75

Social Studies 28

Some Help from Pocahontas

Life was difficult in Jamestown, Virginia. In 1607, English settlers built a town there. But, they couldn't grow or find enough food. The Native Americans often attacked their town. One day, they captured John Smith, the captain of the settlers. The chief of the tribe wanted to kill Smith. His daughter felt mercy and saved Smith. Soon, Smith became friends with the tribe. Pocahontas showed the English the way to grow and find food. She became a symbol of peace between the two groups. Today, we can even see Pocahontas' story in a Disney movie!

Read and Complete

❶ English _____ built a town in Jamestown.

❷ Pocahontas was a daughter of the _____ of the tribe.

Words to Know

- □ **settler** 정착민
- □ **Native American** 미국 원주민
- □ **attack** 공격하다
- □ **capture** 포로로 잡다
- □ **captain** 대장, 대위
- □ **chief** 추장, 족장
- □ **tribe** 부족, 종족
- □ **mercy** 자비, 연민
- □ **symbol** 상징
- □ **peace** 평화

배경지식 Plus!

디즈니의 애니메이션 〈포카혼타스〉에서는 원주민 소녀 포카혼타스가 백인 청년 John Smith와 사랑에 빠지고, 백인과 원주민 간의 전쟁을 막아 평화를 지켜 내지요. 하지만 실제 이야기는 달라요. 포카혼타스는 1613년에 영국인에게 납치되어 인질이 되었어요. 영국인들과 원주민들의 관계는 평탄치 않았고, 포카혼타스는 21살에 천연두에 걸려 죽었다고 해요.

(A) Circle the best answer.

1. What difficulty did the English settlers have?
   - ⓐ growing food
   - ⓑ building towns
   - ⓒ finding friends

2. Who tried to kill John Smith?
   - ⓐ the settlers
   - ⓑ Pocahontas
   - ⓒ the chief of the tribe

3. What is NOT true about the Native Americans?
   - ⓐ They consisted of tribes.
   - ⓑ They often attacked the settlers.
   - ⓒ They wanted to be friends with the settlers.
   - ⓓ They caught the captain of the English settlers.

4. How did Pocahontas help the English settlers? (Choose 2 answers.)
   - ⓐ She saved the captain of the settlers.
   - ⓑ She taught them how to find food.
   - ⓒ She captured the chief of the tribe.
   - ⓓ She built a town in Virginia for them.

(B) Complete the sentences.

Captain John Smith was an English ❶_____ in Virginia. Pocahontas

❷_____ his life, and helped the settlers. She also helped bring

peace between the ❸_____ Americans and the settlers.

Wrap Up Number the sentences in order.

[3] Pocahontas helped an English man.

[ ] The Native Americans attacked English settlers.

[ ] English settlers built a town in Jamestown, Virginia.

[ ] Pocahontas became a symbol of peace.

The Value of Gold

R2_29.mp3

Why is gold more expensive than water? It's because of supply and demand. If many people want to buy a good, then there is high demand. High demand makes something more valuable. Supply is the amount of a good in markets. Low supply of a good makes it more valuable. Many people want to buy gold or water, so both have high demand. Water is everywhere, but there isn't much gold in the world. So, high demand and low supply makes gold more expensive than water.

Read and Complete

❶ Some people want to buy a good, and it is _____.

❷ Gold is _____ because there isn't much of it in the world.

Words to Know

- value 가치
- expensive 비싼
- supply 공급
- demand 수요
- good 상품, 물건
- valuable 귀중한
- the amount of ~의 양
- everywhere 어디에나

배경지식 Plus!

필통을 3,000원에 파는 기업이 있는데 필통 값이 500원으로 떨어졌다고 해봐요. 기업은 손해를 보면서 물건을 팔고 싶지 않기 때문에 **공급(supply)**을 줄일 거예요. 반대로 필통 값이 6,000원으로 오르면 물건을 더 많이 팔고 싶어서 공급을 늘리겠지요. 물건의 가격이 오르면 공급량이 늘어나고, 가격이 내리면 공급량이 줄어드는 것을 '공급의 법칙'이라고 해요.

Comprehension Checkup

(A) Circle the best answer.

1. What is the amount of a good in the market?
   - ⓐ value
   - ⓑ demand
   - ⓒ supply

2. What can make something more valuable?
   - ⓐ low demand
   - ⓑ low supply
   - ⓒ high supply

3. What does high demand for a good mean?
   - ⓐ That good is easy to buy.
   - ⓑ No one wants that good.
   - ⓒ Some people want that good.
   - ⓓ Lots of people want that good.

4. What is NOT true about gold?
   - ⓐ It has low supply.
   - ⓑ Few people want it.
   - ⓒ It has high demand.
   - ⓓ It has more value than water.

(B) Complete the sentences.

Gold is more expensive than water because of low ❶ ....

Both goods have ❷ .... demand, but gold isn't easy to get.

So it's more ❸ ....

Wrap Up   Fill in the blanks.

The Value of Goods

high ❶ ....
: Many people want
to buy.

➕

low ❷ ....

➡️

expensive,
❸ ....
like ❹ ....

| gold | demand | valuable | supply |

79

Folktales in Folklore

R2_30.mp3

Folklore is the stories and traditions of a culture. They are passed down from generation to generation. This helps preserve and continue the culture over time. Folktales are an important part of folklore. Every culture has its own tradition of folktales. In Europe, these stories often begin with, "Once upon a time..." Parents teach their children through these stories. Folktales often teach children lessons about honesty, kindness, or bravery. Some famous folktales include *The Little Red Hen* and *Cinderella*. What folktales have your parents passed down to you?

Read and Complete

❶ _____ is the traditions of a culture.

❷ Folktales contain _____ for children.

Words to Know

- **folktale** 설화, 전설
- **folklore** 민속, 전통 문화
- **pass down** 물려주다, 대물림하다
- **generation** 세대
- **preserve** 보존하다
- **continue** 계속하다, 이어가다
- **over time** 오랜 시간에 걸쳐
- **lesson** 교훈
- **honesty** 정직
- **kindness** 친절
- **bravery** 용기
- ***The Little Red Hen*** 빨간 꼬마 암탉
- ***Cinderella*** 신데렐라

배경지식 Plus!

미국의 **전통 우화(folktale)** 〈The Little Red Hen〉에서 개, 고양이, 생쥐는 낮잠 자는 것만 좋아하고 집안일은 빨간 암탉의 몫이었어요. 빨간 암탉은 열심히 일해서 거둔 밀로 케이크를 구웠어요. 개, 고양이, 생쥐가 나눠 먹자고 했지만 빨간 암탉은 혼자서 키우고 만든 것이니 혼자 먹겠다고 했어요. 그 이후, 친구들도 집안일을 열심히 했다는 이야기예요.

Comprehension Checkup

A Circle the best answer.

1. Who usually tells children folktales?

ⓐ parents   ⓑ teachers   ⓒ lecturers

2. What lessons do folktales often teach children?

ⓐ how to make money   ⓑ how to be smarter   ⓒ how to behave well

3. What is NOT true about folklore?

ⓐ It preserves traditions.

ⓑ It mostly comes from Europe.

ⓒ It is an important part of culture.

ⓓ It is passed down from generation to generation.

4. What can be inferred about folktales from the passage?

ⓐ Folktales have a set format.

ⓑ Europeans especially loved folktales.

ⓒ Each culture has its own famous folktales.

ⓓ *Cinderella* is the most famous folktale in the world.

B Complete the sentences.

Folklore helps ❶＿＿＿＿＿＿＿ the traditions of a culture. Parents teach

their children lessons about honesty and bravery with ❷＿＿＿＿＿＿＿.

This passes down a culture to the next ❸＿＿＿＿＿＿＿.

Wrap Up Fill in the blanks.

Folklore	Folktale	
• ❶＿＿＿＿＿ of a culture	• an important part of	bravery
• pass down from generation to generation	❸＿＿＿＿＿	traditions
• preserve and continue the	• teach children lessons like honesty, kindness, or	folklore
❷＿＿＿＿＿	❹＿＿＿＿＿	culture

WORD REVIEW

(A) Crossword Puzzle

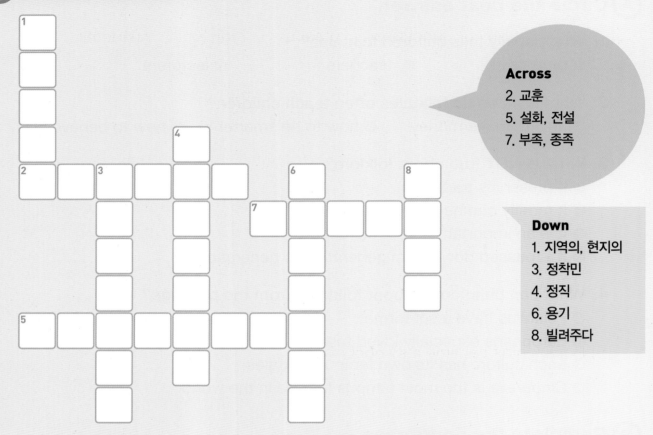

Across
2. 교훈
5. 설화, 전설
7. 부족, 종족

Down
1. 지역의, 현지의
3. 정착민
4. 정직
6. 용기
8. 빌려주다

(B) Match with the correct definition.

1. **demand** •   ⓐ the costs of money / Banks gives you it for your saved money.

2. **folklore** •   ⓑ the need to buy a good or service

3. **interest** •   ⓒ the amount of a good in markets

4. **supply** •   ⓓ the stories and traditions of a culture

C Fill in the blanks with the correct words.

earn	functions	peace	regular	residents

1. Most adults use _____ banks to keep their money.
대부분의 어른들은 돈을 보관하기 위해 일반 은행을 이용합니다.

2. Interest makes both people and banks _____ some money.
이자는 사람들과 은행 둘 다 돈을 벌게 해 줍니다.

3. Making rules is one of the many _____ of a government.
규칙을 만드는 것은 정부의 많은 기능들 중 하나입니다.

4. Local laws are important to the _____ in a certain area.
지역 법은 특정 지역의 주민들에게 중요합니다.

5. Pocahontas became a symbol of _____ between the two groups.
포카혼타스는 두 집단 사이에서 평화의 상징이 되었습니다.

D Fill in the blanks with the correct expressions.

begin with	more ~ than	passed down	pay back
	showed ~ the way		

1. The borrowers must _____ the money on time and pay interest for it to the bank.

2. Pocahontas _____ the English _____ to grow and find food.

3. High demand and low supply makes gold _____ expensive _____ water.

4. In Europe, folktales often _____, "Once upon a time…"

5. What folktales have your parents _____ to you?

Slavery in America

R2_31.mp3

Slavery was common in Colonial America. In the 18th century, plantation owners used African slaves for farmwork. These slaves lived on the plantation and were owned like property.

After working all day in the hot sun, they returned to their huts. The whole family lived and slept on the floors of their small huts. Dinner was often rice, beans, or other plants. Meat was usually only for the plantation owners. Slaves owned few possessions and no money. They just had some blankets for sleeping and dishes for cooking.

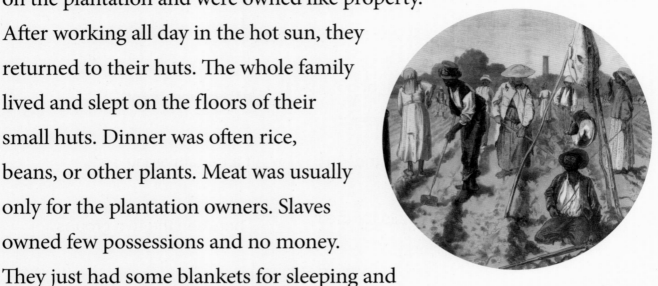

Read and Complete

1 Colonial Americans had many _____.

2 Most of these slaves came from _____.

Words to Know

- slavery 노예 제도, 노예
- common 흔한
- colonial 식민지 시대의
- plantation (열대·아열대 지방의 대규모) 농장
- owner 주인, 소유주
- slave 노예
- own 소유하다
- property 재산
- return 돌아가다
- hut 오두막
- possession 소유물, 재산
- blanket 담요

배경지식 Plus!

미국의 식민지 시대에는 목화와 담배를 길러 유럽에 수출하는 것이 왕성하게 이루어졌어요. 대규모 농장들이 많았는데 기계와 기술이 충분하지 않았기 때문에 어마어마한 노동력이 필요했지요. 농장주들은 흑인 노예들(slaves)을 노동력으로 이용했어요. 노예들은 노예시장에서 사고팔 수 있었고, 임금을 지불하지 않아도 되었기 때문이에요.

Comprehension Checkup

A Circle the best answer.

1. Where did most slaves work?
 ⓐ on a plantation   ⓑ at the owners' huts   ⓒ on the farms in Africa

2. What did slaves receive for their work?
 ⓐ nothing   ⓑ small property   ⓒ small amount of money

3. What is NOT true about slaves' living conditions?
 ⓐ They didn't have enough basic items.
 ⓑ They couldn't eat food of good quality.
 ⓒ They slept on the floors of their small huts.
 ⓓ They were never allowed to have a family.

4. What is true about the plantation owners?
 ⓐ They treated slaves poorly.
 ⓑ They raised farm animals for meat.
 ⓒ They worked during the day with slaves.
 ⓓ They paid some money to support slaves.

B Complete the sentences.

Many slaves lived in ❶_____ America in the 18th century. They were owned like ❷_____ so the owners didn't pay them. They lived and worked on their owners' ❸_____.

Wrap Up Fill in the blanks.

Slavery in America

신분 상태
- ❶_____ in Colonial America in 18th century
- being ❷_____ like property

생활
- working all day
- living in their ❸_____
- eating rice, beans
- few ❹_____

owned

huts

possessions

common

85

R2_32.mp3

Gold Rush in California

John Marshal helped build the State of California. In 1848, he discovered gold in California. The news soon spread around the world. Anyone could find free gold there! At the time, only about 1,000 Americans lived in California. The rush to find gold brought over 300,000 people from around the world there. Most could not find any gold. But many businesses made a lot of money. They sold food, clothes, and equipment to the miners. The miners and businessmen needed roads, churches, and schools. So the government built them.

Read and Complete

❶ John Marshal was the first man to discover _____ in California.

❷ Thousands of people rushed to _____ to find gold.

Words to Know

- **gold rush** 골드러시
- **rush** 급작스럽고 강한 움직임, 쇄도; 급히 움직이다
- **the State of ~** ~주(州)
- **discover** 발견하다
- **spread(-spread)** 퍼지다, 확산되다
- **bring(-brought)** 데려오다
- **business** 사업
- **equipment** 장비
- **miner** 광부
- **businessman** 사업가
- **government** 정부
- **build(-built)** 짓다, 건설하다

배경지식 Plus!

청바지도 골드러시(Gold Rush)로 인해 만들어졌어요. 금을 캐기 위해 캘리포니아에 모여든 사람들은 임시 주거지로 천막을 쳤어요. 리바이 스트라우스는 천막용 천을 만드는 사업을 했는데, 광부들의 바지가 쉽게 해지는 데서 착안하여 천막용 천으로 바지를 만들었어요. 광부들은 튼튼한 이 바지를 즐겨 입게 되었는데 이것이 청바지의 시초가 되었어요.

Comprehension Checkup

(A) Circle the best answer.

1. Before the Gold Rush, how many people lived in California?

    ⓐ about 1,000　　　　ⓑ 1,848　　　　ⓒ about 300,000

2. Who made a lot of money during the Gold Rush?

    ⓐ teachers　　　　ⓑ businessmen　　　　ⓒ the government

3. Why was the news of John Marshal interesting to many people?

    ⓐ Because it made them dream of being rich.

    ⓑ Because he was looking for people to find gold.

    ⓒ Because it helped them become miners.

    ⓓ Because it advertised new jobs in California.

4. What is NOT true about the Gold Rush?

    ⓐ Many people failed to find gold.

    ⓑ It helped build the State of California.

    ⓒ The government hired miners to find gold.

    ⓓ People from around the world came to California.

(B) Complete the sentences.

John Marshal ❶_____ gold in California in 1848. People from around the world came to find gold. During the Gold Rush, ❷_____ that sold food and clothes made lots of ❸_____.

WrapUp Write the numbers in order.

    [3]　Many businesses made a lot of money.

    [   ]　John Marshal discovered gold in California.

    [   ]　The government built roads, churches, and schools.

    [   ]　The rush to find gold brought over 300,000 people.

An Entrepreneur in the Animation Industry

R2_33.mp3

These days, millions of people enjoy animated shows and movies. Walt Disney was the first to create one, and it became popular. He was an entrepreneur with a great idea. He wanted to turn his drawings and characters into a business. TV shows at the time only had real actors in them. His idea was to make TV shows and movies with his animated drawings. But, he was fired and rejected over 300 times before becoming successful! Entrepreneurs like Disney face risks and failure. But they also have opportunities for great success!

Read and Complete

1 Walt Disney was an _____ with great ideas.

2 People still enjoy Walt Disney's _____ movies.

Words to Know

- entrepreneur 사업가, 기업가
- animation 만화 영화
- industry 산업
- millions of 수백만의, 수많은
- animated (사진·그림 등이) 동영상으로 된, 만화 영화로 된
- fire 해고하다
- reject 거절하다
- successful 성공적인
- face 마주하다, 직면하다
- risk 위험, 위기
- failure 실패
- opportunity 기회
- success 성공

배경지식 Plus!

월트 디즈니(Walt Disney)는 어릴 적부터 그림에 소질을 보였어요. 7살 때 신문팔이를 하는 동안 만화를 접하면서 그림과 만화에 대한 꿈을 키웠어요. 그는 고등학교 시절부터 광고 만화를 그렸고, 미술학교 졸업 후 광고용 애니메이션을 만들었어요. 그 후 수많은 좌절과 도전 끝에, 1937년 첫 애니메이션 장편 영화 〈백설공주〉를 개봉하여 대성공을 거두었지요.

Comprehension Checkup

(A) Circle the best answer.

1. What did Walt Disney create first?
   - ⓐ movies
   - ⓑ TV shows
   - ⓒ animated shows

2. What did people see in TV shows before Walt Disney's idea?
   - ⓐ voice actors
   - ⓑ only real actors
   - ⓒ animated drawings

3. What is true about entrepreneurs like Walt Disney?
   - ⓐ They never face risk or failure.
   - ⓑ They sometimes copy old ideas.
   - ⓒ They have opportunities for success.
   - ⓓ They hate watching TV shows and movies.

4. What can you infer about Walt Disney from the passage?
   - ⓐ He wanted to be an actor in a TV show.
   - ⓑ He was interested in drawing characters.
   - ⓒ He was sick and tired of watching TV shows.
   - ⓓ He was rich enough to make his dreams come true.

(B) Complete the sentences.

Walt Disney was a famous entrepreneur. His new ❶............................ was to use animated ❷............................ for TV shows and movies. He succeeded at last after facing ❸............................ and failure.

WrapUp Fill in the blanks.

Entrepreneurs	Walt Disney	
• people with great ideas	• animated TV shows and movies	face
• ❶............ risks and failure	• was ❸............ and rejected	fired
• ❷............ something first	• turned his ❹............ into a business	drawings
		create

89

Women's Right to Vote

R2_34.mp3

Just 100 years ago in America, women had few legal rights. They couldn't vote, own homes, or do most jobs. The women's rights movement began in the 1800s. They fought for equal rights. The right to vote, Women's Suffrage, was their main goal. But, the laws of the United States did not allow them to vote. They formed political groups to change the law. Susan B. Anthony was an important leader of these groups. Because of their efforts, the law was changed. Women now have equal legal rights.

Read and Complete

1 Until about 100 years ago, women in America could not _____.

2 Women worked hard to change the _____.

Words to Know

- **right** 권리
- **vote** 투표하다, 선거하다
- **legal** 법률상의, 합법적인
- **movement** (조직적으로 벌이는) 운동
- **fight(-fought)** 싸우다
- **equal** 동등한, 공평한
- **suffrage** 투표권, 참정권
- **main** 주요한
- **goal** 목표
- **form** 형성하다
- **political** 정치적인
- **leader** 지도자
- **effort** 노력

배경지식 Plus!

교사였던 수잔 B. 앤서니(Susan B. Anthony)는 미국의 남북전쟁 시대에 노예제도 폐지, 금주 운동 등을 주장하며 사회활동에 뛰어들었어요. 또한 여성 권리 쟁취를 목표로 주간지를 발간하며 운동을 펼쳤어요. 그녀는 1872년 실시된 미국 대통령 선거에 여성으로서의 참여를 강행하여 100달러의 벌금형을 부과받기도 했어요.

Comprehension Checkup

A Circle the best answer.

1. What was the purpose of the women's movement in the 1800s?
   - ⓐ to have equal rights
   - ⓑ to fight against men
   - ⓒ to change the president

2. What does Women's Suffrage mean?
   - ⓐ the right to vote
   - ⓑ efforts to own homes
   - ⓒ the right to have jobs

3. What did women do to change the law?
   - ⓐ They left their jobs.
   - ⓑ They made political groups.
   - ⓒ They voted for women.
   - ⓓ They asked men to help them.

4. What is NOT true about the women's movement?
   - ⓐ It helped change the unfair law.
   - ⓑ It gave equal legal rights to women.
   - ⓒ Its main goal was to get the right to have property.
   - ⓓ Susan B. Anthony was the leader of women's groups.

B Complete the sentences.

In the 1800s, the women's rights ❶_____ started to fight for the equal

right to ❷_____. Women formed political groups to ❸_____

the law. Thanks to their efforts, women now have equal legal rights.

Wrap Up   Fill in the blanks.

Women's Rights Movement

100 years ago in America	• Women had few ❶_____ rights.	political
What Women Wanted	• suffrage: the right to ❷_____	vote
What Women Did	• formed ❸_____ groups and changed the law	equal
	• have ❹_____ legal rights now	legal

Balance of Power

R2_35.mp3

Three branches of the American government balance each other's power. The first branch is Congress. Congressmen can create new laws. The next branch is the President. He is the leader of the country. The final branch is the judges. Judges can change or remove laws. Each branch can check the power of the other branches. This makes sure that all three branches follow the law. They even have the power to cancel the actions of other branches. For example, the President can reject new laws of Congress. Congress can even vote to remove judges or the President.

Read and Complete

① The American government is made up of three _____.

② The _____ of the three branches is balanced.

Words to Know

- **balance** 균형; 균형을 유지하다
- **branch** (큰 조직의) 부서, 기관
- **Congress** 의회
- **Congressman** 국회의원
- **president** 대통령
- **leader** 지도자
- **final** 마지막의
- **judge** 판사, 사법부
- **remove** 없애다, 해임하다
- **check** 견제하다; 견제
- **make sure** 반드시 ~하도록 하다
- **reject** 거부하다

배경지식 Plus!

국가에 왕처럼 군림하는 하나의 부서만 있다면 어떨까요? 한 부서에서 법을 정해서 그대로 집행하면 시간과 노력이 많이 들지 않을 테니 효율적일 수 있어요. 하지만 민주주의 국가에서 법을 제정하는 입법부, 집행하는 행정부, 적용하는 사법부로 구성된 삼권분립 체제를 만든 것은 효율성보다는 권력을 분산하여 국민의 권리와 자유를 보장하기 위해서예요.

A Circle the best answer.

1. What do Congressmen do?
   ⓐ make new laws   ⓑ remove laws   ⓒ lead the country

2. How can Congress make sure judges follow the law?
   ⓐ by voting to remove them
   ⓑ by rejecting laws for judges
   ⓒ by asking the President to remove them

3. What is true about the President?
   ⓐ He has the right to break new laws.
   ⓑ He has the power to reject new laws.
   ⓒ His main task is finding problems of laws.
   ⓓ He checks the judges by removing them.

4. Why do the three branches check each other?
   ⓐ Because they try not to influence each other.
   ⓑ Because they have to make sure all of them follow the law.
   ⓒ Because they want to have as much power as possible.
   ⓓ Because they have to discuss new laws.

B Complete the sentences.

The American government has three branches: the ❶_____, Congress,

and the judges. They ❷_____ and ❸_____ each other's power.

Wrap Up   Fill in the blanks.

The American Government

❶_____	❷_____	❸_____
• create new laws • vote to remove judges and presidents	• the leader of the country • can reject new laws	can change or remove laws

A Crossword Puzzle

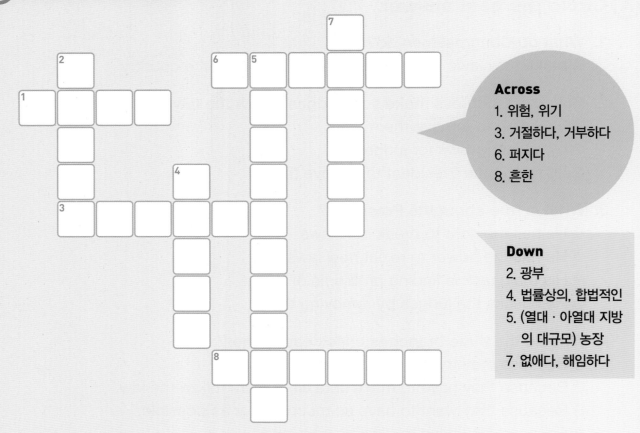

Across
1. 위험, 위기
3. 거절하다, 거부하다
6. 퍼지다
8. 흔한

Down
2. 광부
4. 법률상의, 합법적인
5. (열대 · 아열대 지방의 대규모) 농장
7. 없애다, 해임하다

B Match with the correct definition.

1. entrepreneur •
    ⓐ someone who is owned like property

2. gold rush •
    ⓑ when people around the world went to California to find gold

3. president •
    ⓒ a person who starts or runs a business to make money

4. slave •
    ⓓ the leader of the country

C Fill in the blanks with the correct words.

| businessmen | Colonial | congressmen | political | opportunities |

1. Slavery was common in _____ America in the 18th.

18세기 식민지 시대의 미국에서 노예 제도는 흔한 것이었습니다.

2. _____ sold food, clothes, and equipment to the miners.

사업가들은 광부들에게 음식, 옷, 장비를 판매했습니다.

3. Entrepreneurs have _____ for great success.

사업가들은 큰 성공의 기회를 갖습니다.

4. Women formed _____ groups to change the law.

여성들은 법을 바꾸기 위해 정치 단체를 형성했습니다.

5. _____ can create new laws.

국회의원들은 새로운 법을 만들 수 있습니다.

D Fill in the blanks with the correct expressions.

| allow ~ to | fought for | lived on | make sure | turn ~ into |

1. African slaves _____ the plantation.

2. Walt Disney wanted to _____ his drawings and characters _____ a business.

3. Women _____ equal rights in the 1800s.

4. The laws of the United States did not _____ women _____ vote.

5. Checks and balances _____ all three branches follow the law.

The Trail of Tears

R2_36.mp3

Before 1830, Native Americans lived free in the Southern USA. But, the American population was growing quickly. They wanted to expand into Native American lands. The government passed the Indian Removal Act. This law created the Indian Territory in Oklahoma. This territory was very far away from the Native Americans' homeland. Government soldiers marched the Native Americans thousands of kilometers to their new home. There wasn't much food, and the journey took months. Thousands of Native Americans became sick and died. That's why it's remembered as the Trail of Tears.

Read and Complete

① The Indian _____ Act removed Native Americans from their homes.

② Native Americans _____ thousands of kilometers to their new home.

Words to Know

- **trail** 자취, 오솔길, 루트
- **southern** 남쪽의
- **population** 인구
- **expand** 확장하다, 넓히다
- **pass** (법안 등을) 통과시키다
- **removal** 제거, 없애기
- **act** 법안
- **territory** 영역
- **homeland** 고국, 특정 민족 거주 지역
- **soldier** 군인
- **march** (걷도록 강요해서) 데려가다; 행군하듯 걷다
- **journey** 여행, 여정

배경지식 Plus!

인디언 이주법(Indian Removal Act)에는 동부의 인디언 토지와 미시시피강 서쪽의 토지를 교환하자는 조건이 있었지만, 대부분의 원주민들은 찬성하지 않았어요. 하지만 앤드류 잭슨 대통령이 강제로 집행하여 1830~1850년에 원주민 부족들을 강제로 이주시켰어요. 그 도중에 약 17,000명의 원주민들 중 약 5,000명이 목숨을 잃었다고 해요.

A Circle the best answer.

1. Where did the Native Americans move to?
   a Oklahoma   b Southern USA   c American's territory

2. Who led Native Americans to their new home?
   a Indians   b government soldiers   c the leader of the government

3. Why did the government pass the Indian Removal Act?
   a Because Native Americans often attacked them.
   b Because they wanted to take Native American lands.
   c Because they wanted to live with Native Americans.
   d Because they tried to make Native Americans' lives better.

4. What is NOT true about the Trail of Tears?
   a It was difficult to find enough food.
   b It was thousands of kilometers long.
   c Lots of Native Americans got sick and died.
   d It took years to get Native Americans' new home.

B Complete the sentences.

In 1830, the Indian Removal Act made the ❶_____ Americans move

to new territory. They marched thousands of kilometers. Many people

became sick and ❷_____. So we call it the Trail of ❸_____.

Wrap Up Number the sentences in order.

[3] Native Americans were forced to a new home.

[   ] The government passed the Indian Removal Act.

[   ] Many Native Americans became sick and died during the journey.

[   ] The American population grew quickly.

Choices Have Costs

R2_37.mp3

In economics, opportunity cost is the value you lose when you make a choice. Every choice has a value and a cost. Sometimes we have to decide between two valuable choices. But value and costs are not just measured in money. For example, friendship, education, and happiness all have value. Imagine you should choose to play or study. Both activities are valuable. When you choose to play, you are happy. But the opportunity cost is knowledge. Choosing to study can allow you to gain knowledge, but losing fun is the opportunity cost.

Read and Complete

① Choices often have _____ costs.

② Opportunity cost happens when both choices have _____.

Words to Know

- choice 선택
- economics 경제학
- opportunity cost 기회 비용
- value 가치
- decide 결정하다
- valuable 가치 있는
- measure 측정하다, 재다
- education 교육
- happiness 행복
- imagine 상상하다
- choose 선택하다
- activity 활동
- knowledge 지식
- gain 얻다

배경지식 Plus!

기회 비용(opportunity cost)은 한 가지를 선택함으로써 포기하는 것 중 가장 가치가 큰 것을 의미해요. 모든 선택에는 대가가 따른다는 삶의 원리를 담고 있어요. 인어공주는 다리를 얻는 대신 목소리를 잃었죠. 심청은 아버지의 눈을 뜨게 하는 대신에 목숨을 잃는 쪽을 선택했죠. 여러분의 생활 속에서 발생하는 기회 비용도 생각해 보세요.

Comprehension Checkup

A Circle the best answer.

1. Where did the idea of opportunity cost come from?
   ⓐ science   ⓑ economics   ⓒ mathematics

2. How do we measure opportunity cost?
   ⓐ in time   ⓑ in money   ⓒ in lost value

3. What is the opportunity cost of NOT studying?
   ⓐ losing fun
   ⓑ losing time
   ⓒ being happy
   ⓓ getting knowledge

4. Which choice does NOT have an opportunity cost?
   ⓐ sleeping or having a meal
   ⓑ studying or meeting friends
   ⓒ reducing stress or getting stressed
   ⓓ having a job or going to university

B Complete the sentences.

Opportunity ❶_____ can happen when we make a ❷_____ between two ❸_____ activities. The lost value of our choice is the opportunity cost.

Wrap Up Fill in the blanks.

Opportunity Cost

의미	the value you lose when you make a ❶_____
발생 상황	when you ❷_____ between two valuable choices
성격	Some ❸_____ and costs are not ❹_____ in money.

measured

decide

choice

values

99

Two Kinds of Democracy

R2_38.mp3

Democratic governments are ruled by their citizens. There are two different kinds of democracy. In a direct democracy, citizens meet and vote for every decision of the government. Most countries are too large and their citizens are too busy for a direct democracy. Instead, in a representative democracy, citizens choose government leaders. Citizens vote for leaders in free and fair elections. It's important all citizens have the equal right to vote in a representative democracy. These leaders represent the citizens and make decisions for them. America, France, and India are examples of representative democracies.

Read and Complete

① _____ have power in a democracy.

② In elections, citizens can _____ for their leaders.

Words to Know

- □ **democracy** 민주주의
- □ **democratic** 민주주의의
- □ **rule** 통치하다, 다스리다
- □ **citizen** 시민
- □ **direct** 직접적인
- □ **vote** 투표하다
- □ **decision** 결정
- □ **representative** 대표하는
- □ **fair** 공정한
- □ **election** 선거
- □ **equal** 동등한, 공평한
- □ **right** 권리
- □ **represent** 대표하다
- □ **India** 인도

배경피식 Plus!

고대 그리스와 로마에서는 **직접 민주주의(direct democracy)**를 실행했어요. 아테네에는 '민회'라는 제도가 있었는데 이곳에서 주민들은 누구나 제약 없이 법률을 제안하고 통과시킬 수 있었지요. 하지만 인구가 증가하고 도시가 확장하다 보니 모이기 힘들어지고, 오히려 다수의 정치 참여를 보장하는 것이 어려워지게 됐어요.

Comprehension Checkup

(A) Circle the best answer.

1. How do citizens have power over the government decisions in a direct democracy?
   - (a) by meeting and voting
   - (b) by making other decisions
   - (c) by choosing the government leaders

2. What do the leaders do for citizens in a representative democracy?
   - (a) control citizens' rights
   - (b) make decisions for them
   - (c) gather citizens to vote

3. Why do some countries have a representative democracy?
   - (a) Because most governments don't trust citizens.
   - (b) Because citizens are too busy in most countries.
   - (c) Because citizens hate to make important decisions.
   - (d) Because a good leader can be smarter than citizens.

4. Why does the writer mention America, France, and India?
   - (a) to disagree with direct democracies
   - (b) to explain why elections should be fair
   - (c) to give examples of representative democracies
   - (d) to compare direct and representative democracies

(B) Complete the sentences.

In a ❶_____ democracy, citizens meet and vote for decisions made by the government. On the other hand, citizens ❷_____ for their leaders in a ❸_____ democracy.

Wrap Up Fill in the blanks.

| direct democracy | • Citizens ❶_____ and vote for every ❷_____ of the government. | elections |
| representative democracy | • Citizens ❸_____ government leaders.
• Citizens vote for leaders in free and fair ❹_____. | decision
meet
choose |

R2_39.mp3

For Common Good: The US Constitution

The US Constitution was written in 1787. Its authors included George Washington, Ben Franklin, and other early founders of America. The Constitution is a set of laws. It says how the American government works. The founders imagined a new kind of free society. At that time, some governments in Europe had a powerful king and queen.

Unlike them, the founders believed that governments should have limited power. They designed the Constitution to give citizens control of the government. A limited government and free citizens helped America grow and become powerful.

Read and Complete

① The early founders of America wrote the US _____.

② The founders hoped to make a society with free _____.

Words to Know

- **common** 흔한, 공동의
- **constitution** 헌법
- **author** 저자, 입안자
- **include** 포함하다
- **founder** 창립자, 설립자
- **a set of** 한 세트의, 일련의
- **imagine** 상상하다, 그리다
- **society** 사회
- **believe** 믿다
- **limited** 제한된
- **design** 설계하다
- **control** 통제권

배경지식 Plus!

1776년, 식민지 대표로 구성된 회의가 미국의 독립을 선언했어요. 곧 국민에게 주권이 있음에 동의하는 13개 주가 탄생했어요. 1781년에 영국과의 독립 전쟁에서 승리한 미국 각 주의 대표자들은 상호 유대관계를 강화하기 위한 '연합 규약'을 채택했어요. 1787년에 연합 규약을 수정하기로 하다가 아예 새로운 헌법(constitution)을 만들게 되었어요.

Comprehension Checkup

(A) Circle the best answer.

1. What does the US Constitution tell us?
- ⓐ the way the government functions
- ⓑ how the early founders built the government
- ⓒ how to control the power of a king and a queen

2. What was important for the founders to make a society?
- ⓐ laws
- ⓑ citizens' freedom
- ⓒ a strong government

3. What is true about the American government?
- ⓐ It had limited power.
- ⓑ It was led by citizens from Europe.
- ⓒ A king and a queen controlled it.
- ⓓ Its power was controlled by the early founders.

4. How did the US Constitution help America grow?
- ⓐ by making citizens less powerful
- ⓑ by removing the government system
- ⓒ by giving citizens freedom and power
- ⓓ by designing the powerful government system

(B) Complete the sentences.

In 1787, the early ❶........................ of America wrote the US Constitution. They

❷........................ the Constitution to give more ❸........................ to the citizens.

Wrap Up Fill in the blanks.

The US Constitution

의미	• a set of ❶........................ saying how the American government works	limited
제정 이유	• for a new ❷........................ with freedom	laws
제정 방향	• to give citizens ❸........................ of the government	control
	• a ❹........................ government and free citizens	society

103

Social Studies
40

Human Rights for All

R2_40.mp3

The Bill of Rights allows American citizens to live freely and safely. James Madison created it in 1789. The basic human rights from it are now common in democracies everywhere. One important right is freedom of speech. With this right, citizens cannot be arrested for giving their opinions. They can even protest government decisions. Other human rights make laws fair for citizens. For example, citizens are innocent until judges prove them guilty in modern democracies. Another basic right is freedom of religion. Citizens are free to choose and follow any religion.

Read and Complete

1 The Bill of Rights protects American citizens' basic _____.

2 Human rights are important in _____.

Words to Know

- **human right** 인권
- **the Bill of Rights** 권리장전
- **allow A to B**
  A가 B하도록 허용하다
- **freely** 자유롭게
- **safely** 안전하게
- **freedom** 자유
- **speech** 말, 연설
- **arrest** 체포하다, 구속하다
- **opinion** 의견
- **protest** 항의하다, 반대하다
- **innocent** 무죄의
- **prove** 입증하다
- **guilty** 유죄의
- **modern** 현대의
- **religion** 종교

배경지식 Plus!

권리장전(the Bill of Rights)에는 정부로부터 개인의 권리를 보호하기 위해 다음 항목이 담겨 있어요. 1. 종교, 언론, 출판의 자유 2. 무기 소지의 권리 3. 군대의 의무 4. 영장 없는 수색 및 체포 금지 5. 형사소송에서의 권리 6. 공정하고 공개된 재판을 받을 권리 7. 민사사건에서 배심원 심리 보장 8. 과잉처벌 금지 9. 인민의 일반적 권리 10. 주와 인민이 갖는 권한

Comprehension Checkup

(A) Circle the best answer.

1. What is the purpose of the Bill of Rights?
   ⓐ to create laws   ⓑ to be free from arrest   ⓒ to live safely with freedom

2. What was James Madison's achievement?
   ⓐ making the Bill of Rights   ⓑ making laws of religion
   ⓒ making a process how to prove a person's guilt

3. What is freedom of speech? (Choose 2 answers.)
   ⓐ Citizens can do newspaper work.
   ⓑ Citizens are free to follow any religion.
   ⓒ Citizens can express their opinions freely.
   ⓓ Citizens can protest government decisions.

4. Which is the example of ignoring human rights?
   ⓐ changing one's religion often
   ⓑ gathering to express disagreement
   ⓒ arresting a person before he or she is proved guilty
   ⓓ moving to a new place without anyone's agreement

(B) Complete the sentences.

The Bill of ❶................... protects the rights of American citizens. Human

rights such as freedom of ❷................... and ❸................... are important.

Wrap Up   Fill in the blanks.

the Bill of Rights

만든 시기	James Madison ❶................... it in 1789.	fair
만든 이유	to allow American citizens to live freely and ❷...................	safely
주요 내용	freedom of speech, ❸................... laws for citizens, ❹................... of religion	created / freedom

WORD REVIEW

A Crossword Puzzle

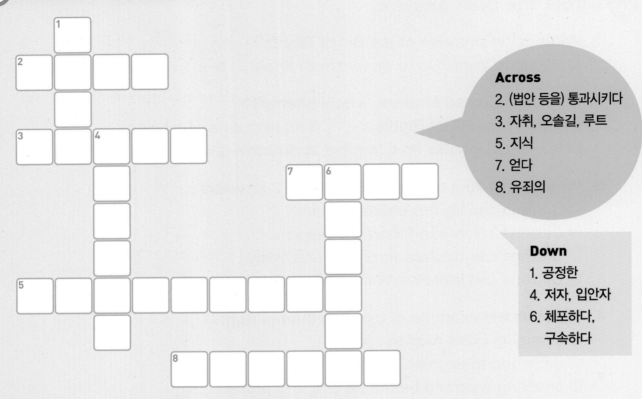

Across
2. (법안 등을) 통과시키다
3. 자취, 오솔길, 루트
5. 지식
7. 얻다
8. 유죄의

Down
1. 공정한
4. 저자, 입안자
6. 체포하다, 구속하다

B Match with the correct definition.

1. election •
   ⓐ the value you lose when you make a choice

2. innocent •
   ⓑ a fair way for citizens to choose government leaders

3. opportunity cost •
   ⓒ a set of laws

4. constitution •
   ⓓ not guilty

Ⓒ Fill in the blanks with the correct words.

| imagined | marched | measured | protest | represent |

1. Government soldiers _____ the Native Americans thousands of kilometers to their new home.

정부군은 북미 원주민들을 새로운 집으로 향하는 수천 킬로미터를 강제로 걷게 했습니다.

2. Value and costs are not just _____ in money.

가치와 비용은 돈으로만 측정되지는 않습니다.

3. The leaders _____ the citizens and make decisions for them.

대표자들은 시민들을 대표하고 그들을 위한 결정을 합니다.

4. The founders _____ a new kind of free society.

설립자들은 새로운 종류의 자유로운 사회를 상상했습니다.

5. Citizens can even _____ government decisions.

시민들은 정부의 결정에 대해서 항의할 수도 있습니다.

Ⓓ Fill in the blanks with the correct expressions.

| are free to | expand into | give ~ control | have to | vote for |

1. Americans wanted to _____ Native American lands.

2. Sometimes we _____ decide between two valuable choices.

3. Citizens _____ leaders in free and fair elections.

4. They designed the Constitution to _____ citizens _____ of the government.

5. Citizens _____ choose and follow any religion.

Music
41

All American Sound

R2_41.mp3

Can you play the banjo? How about the guitar? Both are string instruments. Sounds are made by plucking their strings. Thicker or longer strings make lower sounds. Thinner or shorter strings make higher sounds. Banjos and guitars sound different though. That's because banjos have a different body than guitars. The body of a banjo is round and looks like a drum. This produces a unique sound. It is popular in traditional American music. You can hear that sound in a song like "Old Suzanna."

Read and Complete

❶ Banjos and guitars are _____ instruments.

❷ Banjos' sound is popular in traditional American _____.

Words to Know

- **banjo** 밴조 (악기)
- **string** (악기의) 현, 줄
- **string instrument** 현악기
- **pluck** (현·줄을) 뜯다, 퉁기다
- **though** 그렇지만, 하지만
- **look like** ~처럼 보이다
- **produce** 만들어 내다
- **unique** 독특한, 고유의
- **popular** 인기 있는
- **traditional** 전통의
- **performance** 공연

배경지식 Plus!

밴조(banjo)는 재즈나 민속 음악에 쓰이는 기타의 일종으로 아랍이나 유럽의 기타가 아프리카로 건너가서 변형된 것으로 추정해요. 서아프리카에서 바니아(bania)라고 지칭하던 것을 흑인들이 미국으로 가져와서 밴조가 되었다고 해요. 목 부분이 길고, 탬버린처럼 둥근 모양의 틀에 가죽이 씌워져 있어요. 줄은 4현부터 9현까지 다양하답니다.

(A) Circle the best answer.

1. What kind of strings makes higher sounds?
    (a) long strings   (b) short strings   (c) thick strings

2. What causes the different sound between banjos and guitars?
    (a) body shapes   (b) how to play   (c) how popular it is

3. What is true about a banjo?
    (a) It looks like a guitar.
    (b) It sounds like a drum.
    (c) American people love its unique sound.
    (d) Its thinner strings make lower sounds.

4. Why does the writer mention "Old Suzanna"?
    (a) to compare banjos and guitars
    (b) to explain the history of American music
    (c) to show the great performance with banjos
    (d) to give an example of music with banjos

(B) Complete the sentences.

Guitars and banjos are both string ❶_____. They look different, so they ❷_____ different sounds. Banjos are ❸_____ in traditional American music.

Wrap Up   Fill in the blanks.

Banjo		
소리 내는 방법	• by plucking their ❶_____	
음역	• thin and short strings: high sound	
	• thick and long strings: ❷_____ sound	
특별한 점	• produce a ❸_____ sound	
	• popular in ❹_____ American music	

unique

low

strings

traditional

Are You in 2D or 3D Shape?

R2_42.mp3

You and I have three dimensions (3D). In other words, we have height, length, and width. But a picture or drawing of you only has two dimensions (2D). It only has height and length. The same is true for some shapes, and they can be either 3D or 2D. Sometimes, you can take a 2D shape and add width to make a 3D shape. If you give a square width, it becomes a cube. A 2D circle becomes a 3D sphere. What are some other 3D shapes?

Read and Complete

① 3D shapes have _____, length, and width.

② Shapes can be 2 or 3 _____.

Words to Know
- □ **dimension** 차원, 관점
- □ **in other words** 다시 말해서
- □ **height** 높이, 키
- □ **length** 길이
- □ **width** 너비
- □ **either A or B** A이거나 B
- □ **add** 더하다
- □ **cube** 정육면체
- □ **sphere** 구

배경지식 Plus!

보통의 잉크젯 프린터 같은 2D 프린터가 활자나 그림을 인쇄한다면, **3D(three dimensions)** 프린터는 입력한 도면을 바탕으로 3차원의 입체 형태를 만들어 내는 기계예요. 2D 프린터는 앞뒤(x축)와 좌우(y축)로만 움직이지만, 3D 프린터는 여기에 상하(z축) 움직임을 더하여 입체 형태를 만들어 냅니다.

(A) Circle the best answer.

1. What is an example of a 2D shape?
   - ⓐ a cube
   - ⓑ a sphere
   - ⓒ a square

2. How can you change a 2D shape into a 3D shape?
   - ⓐ by adding length
   - ⓑ by adding width
   - ⓒ by adding height

3. Why does the writer mention "a picture of you"?
   - ⓐ to explain the meaning of 3D
   - ⓑ to give an example of 2 dimensions
   - ⓒ to describe how to make 3D shapes
   - ⓓ to prove 2D shapes are more natural than 3D shapes

4. What is NOT true about 2D and 3D?
   - ⓐ Drawings of something have two dimensions.
   - ⓑ If you give a circle width, it becomes a sphere.
   - ⓒ Shapes in 2 dimensions have height and length.
   - ⓓ If you take width away from a square, it becomes a cube.

(B) Complete the sentences.

❶ _____ in 2 dimensions have height and ❷ _____.

If we add ❸ _____ to a 2D shape, it can be a shape in

3 dimensions.

Wrap Up Fill in the blanks.

| 2 dimensions | — | height, ❶ _____ | — | ❷ _____, circle |

| 3 dimensions | — | height, length, ❸ _____ | — | cube, ❹ _____ |

width   length   sphere   square

Is That Number Prime or Composite?

R2_43.mp3

We can count whole numbers. Whole numbers greater than 1 can either be prime or composite numbers. How do we distinguish between prime numbers and composite numbers? It's easy! Prime numbers can only be divided without remainder by 1 or the prime number itself. Is 3 a prime number? Yes, because 3 can only be divided without remainder by 1 or 3. How about 4? Is it a prime number? No, because 4 can also be divided by 2 without remainder. It is a composite number. Is 5 a prime or composite number?

Prime Numbers

2	3	5	7	11
13	17	19	23	29
31	37	41	43	47
53	59	61	67	71
73	79	83	89	97

Read and Complete

1 We are able to _____ whole numbers.

2 Whole numbers are either _____ or composite.

Words to Know

- **prime number** 소수(1과 자신의 수 외에는 나눌 수 없는 숫자)
- **composite number** 합성수, 비소수
- **count** 세다, 계산하다
- **whole number** 정수
- **distinguish** 구분하다, 구별하다
- **divide** 나누다
- **remainder** 나머지

배경지식 Plus!

0, 1, 2, 3… 등 수를 세거나 순서를 매길 때 사용하는 수를 '자연수'라고 해요. 자연수는 소수(prime number)와 합성수(composite number)로 나누어져요. 소수는 1과 자기 자신으로만 나누어지는 수이고, 그 외 2개 이상의 수로 나누어지는 수는 합성수예요. 자연수보다 좀더 큰 개념은 '음수(−1, −2, −3…)'와 '양수(1, 2, 3…)'를 포함하는 '정수'입니다.

A Circle the best answer.

1. What is an example of a prime number?
     ⓐ 0   ⓑ 7   ⓒ 8

2. What is an example of a composite number?
     ⓐ 3   ⓑ 5   ⓒ 6

3. What can prime numbers be divided without remainder by?
     ⓐ They can be divided by any number.
     ⓑ They can be divided by any prime number.
     ⓒ They can be divided by any composite number.
     ⓓ They can be divided by the prime number itself.

4. What is NOT true about composite numbers?
     ⓐ They are whole numbers.
     ⓑ They include numbers like 9.
     ⓒ They can only be divided by 1 without remainder.
     ⓓ They can be divided by more than 2 numbers.

B Complete the sentences.

Prime and ❶_____ numbers are ❷_____ numbers. Prime

numbers can only be ❸_____ by 2 numbers without remainder.

Composite numbers can be divided by more than 2 numbers without

remainder.

Wrap Up   Fill in the blanks.

❶_____ Numbers

prime numbers	composite ❸_____
can be divided by only 1 or the prime number ❷_____	can be divided by ❹_____ than 2 numbers without remainder

more   whole   numbers   itself

A Story About Seasons

R2_44.mp3

The Ancient Greeks had a story about how Demeter* changed the seasons. There was only one season before this story. Demeter was goddess of the harvest. Long ago, the god Hades* fell in love with Demeter's daughter, Persephone*. But she didn't love him back. He took Persephone to the underworld. Demeter was upset so she didn't allow any plants to grow. Hades agreed to let Persephone return for six months every year. During those six months, Demeter was happy and everything grew. People call this season summer. People call the season when nothing grows winter.

*Demeter 데메테르(농업의 여신) Hades 하데스(죽음과 지하 세계를 관장하는 신) Persephone 페르세포네(저승의 여신)

Read and Complete

❶ Hades loved Persephone, Demeter's _____.

❷ Demeter was _____ because Hades took Persephone away.

Words to Know

- ancient 고대의
- Greek 그리스인
- goddess 여신
- harvest 추수, 수확
- fall in love with
  ~와 사랑에 빠지다
- underworld 지하 세계
- agree 동의하다
- return 돌아오다

배경지식 Plus!

페르세포네의 아버지인 제우스는 하데스(Hades)에게 딸을 돌려줄 것을 요구했어요. 하데스는 페르세포네를 지상으로 보내기 전에 석류의 씨를 먹였어요. 지하 세계의 음식을 먹은 대가로 페르세포네는 지상으로 완전히 돌아가지 못하는 처지가 되었어요. 한 해의 절반은 지하 세계에서 하데스와 지내고, 나머지 절반은 지상에서 데메테르와 함께 지내게 된 것이죠.

Comprehension Checkup

(A) Circle the best answer.

1. What is this Greek story mainly about?
   - ⓐ mother and daughter
   - ⓑ seasons
   - ⓒ underworld

2. Where did Hades take Persephone?
   - ⓐ to Greece
   - ⓑ to Demeter
   - ⓒ to the underworld

3. What is NOT true about Demeter?
   - ⓐ She fell in love with Hades.
   - ⓑ She was goddess of the harvest.
   - ⓒ She stopped plants from growing.
   - ⓓ She was happy when her daughter returned.

4. Why do plants only grow during summer?
   - ⓐ Because Demeter was upset during the summer.
   - ⓑ Because Hades allowed plants to grow only for six months.
   - ⓒ Because Demeter let plants grow while Persephone came back.
   - ⓓ Because Persephone was in the underworld during the summer.

(B) Complete the sentences.

Hades took Persephone to the underworld. Angry Demeter made nothing

❶.............................. This season is ❷.............................. Hades let Persephone return

for six months a year. Then, Demeter allowed everything to grow. This

season is ❸...........................

Wrap Up   Write the numbers in order.

| 5 | Demeter was happy and everything grew during those six months. |

☐ Hades fell in love with Persephone.

☐ Demeter was upset and didn't let any plants grow.

☐ Hades took Persephone to the underworld.

☐ Hades agreed to let Persephone return for six months every year.

A Joyful Day of the Dead

R2_45.mp3

In Mexico, the Day of the Dead is an important holiday. Families gather together to remember their ancestors. On this day, they believe the spirits of the dead can join their families again. It may sound sad and a bit scary, but it's a joyful celebration. Families make altars in their homes. Then, they put their ancestors' favorite food and drinks there. After that, they bring gifts to their ancestors' graves. Often, they wear ghost or skeleton costumes. On the Day of the Dead, the cemeteries are full of celebration!

Read and Complete

❶ The Day of the Dead is a holiday in _____.

❷ Families get together to remember their _____.

Words to Know

□ **joyful** 기쁜

□ **the dead** 망자, 고인

□ **gather** 모이다

□ **ancestor** 조상, 선조

□ **spirit** 영혼

□ **celebration**
축하 행사, 기념 행사

□ **altar** 제단

□ **grave** 무덤

□ **ghost** 유령, 귀신

□ **skeleton** 해골

□ **costume** 의상, 복장

□ **cemetery** 묘지

배경피식 Plus!

멕시코인들은 세상을 떠난 이들이 **망자의 날(Day of the Dead)**에 가족과 친구들을 만나러 세상에 내려온다고 믿어요. 10월 말일에 제단을 마련한 후 11월 1일에는 죽은 아이들을, 11월 2일에는 죽은 어른들을 위해 기도해요. 설탕이나 초콜릿으로 해골 조형물과 뼈 모양 사탕 등을 만들어 제단에 올리기도 한답니다.

(A) Circle the best answer.

1. Where do some families make altars?
   ⓐ on graves   ⓑ in their homes   ⓒ in cemeteries

2. On the Day of the Dead, what joins their families again?
   ⓐ elderly people   ⓑ scary ghosts   ⓒ the spirits of the dead

3. What is NOT true about the Day of the Dead?
   ⓐ It is a sad day for Mexican families.
   ⓑ People often wear special costumes.
   ⓒ People bring gifts to their ancestors' cemeteries.
   ⓓ Food and drinks for ancestors are put on altars.

4. What can be inferred from the passage?
   ⓐ Mexicans hate to feel sadness.
   ⓑ Mexicans believe in the life after death.
   ⓒ The symbols of ghosts are popular in Mexico.
   ⓓ Graves in Mexico are bigger than graves in other countries'.

(B) Complete the sentences.

In Mexico, many families celebrate the Day of the ❶_____.

It is an important ❷_____ because families ❸_____ to

remember their ancestors with joy.

WrapUp Fill in the blanks.

The Day of the Dead		
의미	Families gather and remember ancestors.	costumes
특별한 점	The ❶_____ of the dead join again. ▸ a ❷_____ celebration	joyful spirits
하는 일	make ❸_____, bring gifts to graves, wear ❹_____	altars

WORD REVIEW

(A) Crossword Puzzle

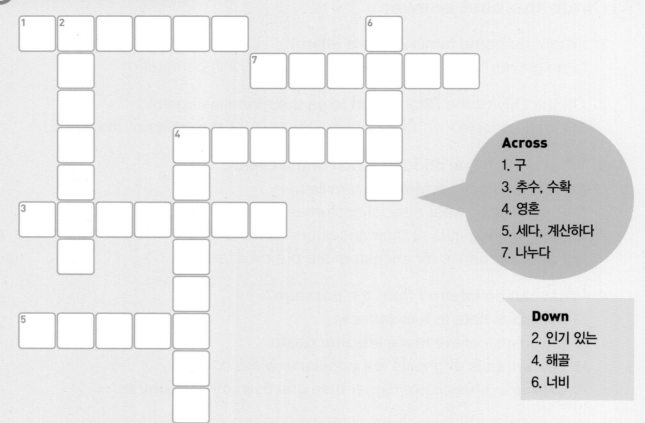

Across
1. 구
3. 추수, 수확
4. 영혼
5. 세다, 계산하다
7. 나누다

Down
2. 인기 있는
4. 해골
6. 너비

(B) Match with the correct definition.

1. composite number •

   ⓐ an instrument that makes a sound when its strings are vibrated

2. prime number •

   ⓑ height, length, and width

3. string instrument •

   ⓒ a number that can only be divided by 1 or itself

4. three dimensions •

   ⓓ a number that can be divided by more than 2 numbers without remainder

C Fill in the blanks with the correct words.

| add | agreed | altars | gather | underworld |

1. You can take a 2D shape and _____ width to make a 3D shape.
여러분은 2D 형태를 가져다가 3D 형태를 만들기 위해 너비를 더할 수 있습니다.

2. Hades took Persephone to the _____.
하데스는 페르세포네를 지하 세계로 데려갔습니다.

3. Hades _____ to let Persephone return for six months every year.
하데스는 페르세포네를 매년 6개월간 돌려보내 주기로 동의했습니다.

4. Families _____ together to remember their ancestors.
가족들은 조상들을 기억하기 위해 함께 모입니다.

5. Families make _____ in their homes.
가족들은 집에 제단을 만듭니다.

D Fill in the blanks with the correct expressions.

| are full of | between ~ and | either ~ or |
| fell in love with | looks like |

1. The body of a banjo is round and _____ a drum.

2. The same is true for some shapes, they can be _____ 3D _____ 2D.

3. How do we distinguish _____ prime numbers _____ composite numbers?

4. The god Hades _____ Demeter's daughter, Persephone.

5. On the Day of the Dead, the cemeteries _____ celebration.

46

R2_46.mp3

Country Music Is Still Alive

Millions of Americans love country music. It's a popular genre of music. It first appeared around 100 years ago with traditional folk music from Ireland and Scotland. And then, it changed and mixed with other cultures when Europeans moved into North America. Folk music usually uses guitars and banjos. Modern country music still uses these instruments. The songs tell stories about life outside of big cities. The lyrics are about romance, struggles, pride, and traditions. In America, country music continues to grow and change, and it is still popular today!

Read and Complete

❶ Country is a popular _____ of music.

❷ Modern country music is still growing and _____.

Words to Know

□ **country music** 컨트리 음악
□ **genre** 장르
□ **appear** 나타나다, 발생하다
□ **folk music** 민요, 민속 음악
□ **Ireland** 아일랜드
□ **Scotland** 스코틀랜드
□ **European** 유럽인
□ **lyrics** 노랫말, 가사
□ **romance** 로맨스, 사랑
□ **struggle** 투쟁, 분투
□ **pride** 자부심, 긍지

배경지식 Plus!

1920년대 유럽에서 북미 지역으로 이주해 온 이민자들이 유럽의 악기와 음악을 가져왔어요. 북미의 다양한 문화와 교류하고 반응하며 독특한 음악이 탄생하게 되지요. 그것이 바로 **컨트리 음악(country music)**이에요. 1950년대에 컨트리 음악이 큰 인기를 얻으며 다른 음악 장르와 혼합된 '컨트리 소울', '컨트리 록' 등의 새로운 장르도 생겨났어요.

Comprehension Checkup

A Circle the best answer.

1. Where did country music first appear?

    ⓐ Ireland   ⓑ North America   ⓒ big cities in America

2. Which instrument does folk music usually NOT use?

    ⓐ banjo   ⓑ violin   ⓒ guitar

3. What is country music NOT about?

    ⓐ missing Africa

    ⓑ pride and traditions

    ⓒ romance and struggles

    ⓓ life outside of big cities

4. What is true about country music?

    ⓐ It means folk songs from Ireland.

    ⓑ It's still very popular in North America.

    ⓒ It is almost the same as traditional folk music.

    ⓓ It failed to interest the new generations.

B Complete the sentences.

❶ _____ music is popular in ❷ _____ America. Country music grew and ❸ _____ over time.

Wrap Up   Fill in the blanks.

Country Music		
유래	• traditional ❶ _____ music from Ireland and Scotland	traditions
주요 악기	• guitars, ❷ _____	life
다루는 주제	• ❸ _____ outside of big cities • romance, struggles, pride, and ❹ _____	banjos folk

Art
47
Wonderful Towers of Watts

R2_47.mp3

Simon Rodia created impressive art by finding objects himself and using only them. In Watts, California, he created sculptures and structures from garbage. He collected it because he didn't have much money. Rodia did all of this work alone, and with simple tools. He was passionate about his artwork. He spent 34 years working on it! His work eventually covered an 800-meter-long area of Watts. He made many tall structures in this area. The tallest was over 30 meters high! Today, the Watts Towers is a popular outdoor museum.

Read and Complete

1 Simon Rodia made the Watts Towers from _____.

2 These days, people enjoy his work as an outdoor _____.

Words to Know

- **impressive** 인상적인
- **object** 물건
- **sculpture** 조각품
- **structure** 구조물
- **garbage** 쓰레기
- **collect** 모으다
- **tool** 도구
- **passionate** 열정적인
- **artwork** 예술 작품
- **eventually** 결국, 마침내
- **outdoor** 야외의

배경지식 Plus!

가족과 헤어져 외롭게 살던 **사이먼 로디아(Simon Rodia)**는 빈민층이 살던 Watts에서 타워를 짓기 시작했어요. 그는 철근, 도자기, 타일, 유리조각, 조개 껍질 등 직접 구한 재료를 이용했어요. 1956년 LA에서 타워가 흉물이라며 철거하려 했지만, 전세계 사람들이 와츠 타워를 지키기 위해 노력한 결과 아직도 유명한 관광명소로 남아 있답니다.

Comprehension Checkup

A. Circle the best answer.

1. How did Rodia get objects to make artworks?
- ⓐ by collecting them himself
- ⓑ by buying them from neighbors
- ⓒ by borrowing them from museums

2. How long did Rodia work on his art?
- ⓐ 800 days
- ⓑ 30 months
- ⓒ 34 years

3. How did Rodia work? (Choose 2 answers.)
- ⓐ He worked very slowly.
- ⓑ He used only garbage.
- ⓒ He worked by himself.
- ⓓ He spent money for objects.

4. What is NOT true about Rodia's artworks in Watts?
- ⓐ They are still popular today.
- ⓑ There are many structures in Watts.
- ⓒ The tallest tower is over 30 meters high.
- ⓓ They covered an 800-meter-long area of the museum.

B. Complete the sentences.

Simon Rodia used garbage and simple ❶_____ to create tall towers. It is the Watts ❷_____ in California. It took 34 ❸_____ for him to finish them.

Wrap Up Fill in the blanks.

Towers of Watts		
재료	❶_____ and use garbage	
작업 방법	work ❷_____, use ❸_____ tools	
작업 기간	34 years	
작품들	the Watts Towers: a popular ❹_____ museum	

outdoor

alone

simple

collect

Understanding Idioms

R2_48.mp3

Idioms are creative and common ways to express language in a certain culture. You cannot understand idioms simply by knowing grammar or the words in the idiom. You can only understand them by their popular use. What does it mean when someone kicked the bucket? It usually doesn't mean literally that a person really kicked a bucket. It means that someone died. Here's another idiom: I hit the books! The literal meaning is that I punched the books. It really means that I studied. What do you think "spill the beans" means? It means to reveal a secret!

Read and Complete

❶ _____ are commonly understood in a certain culture.

❷ "Don't spill the beans" means, "Don't reveal a _____."

Words to Know

- □ idiom 관용구, 숙어
- □ creative 창의적인
- □ express 표현하다
- □ language 언어
- □ grammar 문법
- □ use 사용, 용도
- □ bucket 양동이
- □ literally 문자/말 그대로
- □ literal 문자/말 그대로의
- □ punch 주먹으로 치다
- □ spill 쏟다
- □ bean 콩
- □ reveal 드러내다, 밝히다
- □ secret 비밀

배경지식 Plus!

영어에는 신체 부위와 관련된 **관용구(idiom)**가 많아요. Don't pull Steve's leg.는 'Steve를 놀리지 마.'라는 의미예요. Mary has a big mouth.는 'Mary는 다른 사람 험담을 잘해.'라는 의미이고요. I have butterflies in my stomach.은 I'm so nervous.와 같은 뜻이에요. 관용구가 상황이나 감정을 좀 더 생생하게 표현하는 느낌이 들지요?

(A) Circle the best answer.

1. What does "He kicked the bucket" mean?

　(a) He died.　　　(b) He is angry.　　　(c) He kicked the trash can.

2. When you're studying, which idiom can express your situation?

　(a) I'm spilling the beans.　　　　(b) I'm punching the books.

　(c) I'm hitting the books.

3. What is NOT true about idioms?

　(a) They are not used literally.

　(b) They are creative and popular.

　(c) They are common in language.

　(d) They often use wrong grammar.

4. You want to make sure your friends keep a secret. Which idiom can you use?

　(a) Don't spill the beans.　　　　(b) Don't kick the bucket.

　(c) I hope you spill the beans.　　　(d) I want you to kick the bucket.

(B) Complete the sentences.

Idioms are ❶ _____ and common expressions. They are different

from their ❷ _____ meaning. You can understand idioms by their

popular ❸ _____ .

Wrap Up Fill in the blanks.

Idioms		
특징	• ❶ _____ and common ways to express language in a certain ❷ _____ • understand them by their popular ❸ _____ • not a literal ❹ _____	culture meaning creative use
예시	• kick the bucket, hit the books, spill the beans	

Art 49

Painting with Points

R2_49.mp3

Pointillism is a creative way to paint pictures. It uses dots or points of color to create images. If you look closely, you can see many individual points. If you look from far away, it looks like a regular painting. That's because the points of color appear to blend together. Georges Seurat was a French artist, and he created Pointillism in the 1800s. He made some famous paintings, such as *The Circus*. It describes the circus performers and people watching them. And, it is made up of countless colored dots!

The Circus

Read and Complete

1 _____ of color can create images in Pointillism.

2 Many individual points appear to _____ together.

Words to Know

- **painting** (물감으로 그린) 그림
- **point** 점
- **Pointillism** 점묘법(작은 색점들을 찍어서 표현하는 화법)
- **dot** 점
- **image** 이미지, 그림
- **closely** 가까이서
- **individual** 각각의
- **far away** 멀리 떨어져
- **blend** 섞다
- **circus** 서커스
- **describe** 묘사하다, 서술하다
- **performer** 연기자
- **countless** 셀 수 없이 많은

배경지식 Plus!

조르주 쇠라(George Seurat)는 1880년대에 동료 화가 폴 시냑(Paul Signac)과 함께 점묘법을 개발하며 주목을 받기 시작했어요. 그의 대표작인 '그랑트자트 섬의 일요일 오후'는 작업 기간이 자그마치 2년이나 걸렸어요. 그 정도로 점묘법으로 그림을 그리는 것은 긴 시간과 많은 끈기를 필요로 한다고 해요.

Comprehension Checkup

A Circle the best answer.

1. What do artists use in Pointillism?
    ⓐ dots of colors   ⓑ blended images   ⓒ creative pictures

2. What is the painting *The Circus* about?
    ⓐ countless colors   ⓑ a music performance   ⓒ performers of a circus

3. What is the creative feature of Pointillism?
    ⓐ Artists can express anything with one color.
    ⓑ It looks different based on how far away it is.
    ⓒ Paintings of Pointillism should be looked at closely.
    ⓓ Points of color look different when they're upside down.

4. What is NOT true about Georges Seurat?
    ⓐ He was from France.
    ⓑ He was the first artist of Pointillism.
    ⓒ He used only one color in his paintings.
    ⓓ One of his famous paintings is *The Circus*.

B Complete the sentences.

❶_____ was created in the 1800s by Georges Seurat. Artists can express anything with dots of ❷_____. *The Circus* is one of the most famous ❸_____ in Pointillism.

Wrap Up   Fill in the blanks.

Pointillism		
사용 기법	• ❶_____ or points of color	
효과	• look ❷_____ ▸ many ❸_____ points	
	• look from ❹_____ ▸ a regular painting	
대표 작가	• Georges Seurat ▸ created Pointillism	

far away

individual

closely

dots

The Declaration of Independence

R2_50.mp3

Long ago, America was a British colony. But the American colonists were angry at the British government. That's because they never respected Americans. So on July 4, 1776, Thomas Jefferson wrote The Declaration of Independence. Let's take a look at part of it. "All men are equal and certain basic rights support them. These are life, liberty, and the pursuit of happiness." Also, the Declaration stated why Americans should be independent. It said that Britain had no right to govern Americans. Following the Declaration of Independence, America started its fight for freedom.

Read and Complete

① Britain made America its _____.

② The Americans wanted _____ from Britain.

Words to Know

- **The Declaration of Independence** (미국의) 독립 선언서
- **British** 영국의, 영국인의
- **colony** 식민지
- **colonist** 식민지 주민
- **respect** 존중하다
- **support** 지원하다, 뒷받침하다
- **liberty** 자유
- **pursuit** 추구
- **state** 서술하다
- **independent** 독립된, 독립적인
- **Britain** 영국
- **govern** 다스리다, 지배하다

배경지식 Plus!

미국이 영국으로부터의 **독립(independence)**을 열망하게 된 배경은 무엇이었을까요? 첫 번째로, 영국이 미국 식민지에 과도한 세금을 부과하는 정책을 펼쳤기 때문이에요. 두 번째로, 비옥한 오하이오강 주변 지역으로의 진출을 꿈꾸던 미국인들의 기대와는 달리 영국이 그 지역을 인디언 보호구역으로 선정했기 때문이에요.

Comprehension Checkup

(A) Circle the best answer.

1. What is NOT included in the Declaration of Independence?
   ⓐ the right to protest   ⓑ the right to be free   ⓒ the right to be happy

2. What did Americans let Britain know through the Declaration?
   ⓐ the rights all people should have   ⓑ Americans' excellence
   ⓒ their right to govern the British

3. Why were the colonists upset at the British government?
   ⓐ Because they didn't value Americans.
   ⓑ Because they arrested Thomas Jefferson.
   ⓒ Because they kept expanding their colony.
   ⓓ Because they couldn't speak American English.

4. What happened right after The Declaration of Independence?
   ⓐ America made a new country.
   ⓑ Britain destroyed America.
   ⓒ America became the biggest colony of Britain.
   ⓓ Americans began to protest against the British.

(B) Complete the sentences.

In 1776, American ❶_____ declared independence from Britain.

According to their declaration, all men are ❷_____ and have basic

rights. Also, they didn't want the British to ❸_____ America anymore.

Wrap Up Fill in the blanks.

The Declaration of Independence

날짜	• written on July 4, 1776
목적	• to state American's independence from ❶_____
내용	• All men are ❷_____. • They have basic rights like life, ❸_____, and the ❹_____ of happiness.

equal

liberty

pursuit

Britain

WORD REVIEW

A Crossword Puzzle

Across
2. 노랫말, 가사
3. 자부심, 긍지
4. 존중하다
6. 장르

Down
1. 문자/말 그대로의
5. 비밀
7. 드러내다, 밝히다
8. 물건

B Match with the correct definition.

1. country music •

   ⓐ a popular genre of music played on guitars and banjos.

2. idiom •

   ⓑ a creative and common way to express language in a certain culture

3. independent •

   ⓒ a creative way to paint pictures using points of color

4. Pointillism •

   ⓓ not being governed by others

ⓒ Fill in the blanks with the correct words.

| countless | govern | grammar | passionate | outside |

1. The songs tell stories about life _____ of big cities.

노래는 대도시 밖에서의 삶에 대해 이야기합니다.

2. Simon Rodia was _____ about his artwork.

사이먼 로디아는 예술 작품에 열정적이었습니다.

3. People cannot understand idioms by _____ or words.

사람들은 관용어를 문법이나 단어로 이해할 수 없습니다.

4. *The Circus* is made up of _____ colored dots.

'서커스'는 셀 수 없이 많은 색 점들로 구성되어 있습니다.

5. The Declaration of Independence said that Britain had no right to _____ Americans.

독립 선언서에는 영국이 미국인을 다스릴 권한이 없다고 쓰여 있었습니다.

ⓓ Fill in the blanks with the correct expressions.

| appear to | continues to | the pursuit of | working on | such as |

1. In America, country music _____ grow and change.

2. Simon Rodia spent 34 years _____ his artwork.

3. That's because the points of color _____ blend together.

4. Georges Seurat made some famous paintings, _____ *The Circus*.

5. Basic rights are life, liberty, and _____ happiness.

최신 개정 미국교과서로 독해 실력을 쑥쑥!

미국교과서 READING 시리즈!

| 유치~초등 초급 | 초등 초급 | 초등 중급 | 초등 고급 | 중등 이상 |

단계	Early (전 3권)	Starter (전 3권)	Easy (전 3권)	Basic (전 3권)	Advanced (전 3권)
대상	유치 ~ 초등 초급	초등 초급	초등 중급	초등 고급	중등
특징	기초 어휘와 패턴 문장으로	흥미로운 주제로 픽션&논픽션을	교과서 지식과 독해 실력을 동시에 쌓기 (논픽션)		
난이도 word counting	30~40단어	40~60단어	60~80단어	90~120단어	130~180단어

함께 보면 좋은 책

미국 초등교과서에서 뽑은 콘텐츠를 듣고 받아쓰며
리스닝 실력은 물론 말하기·쓰기·읽기의 통합적 영어 실력을 키웁니다.

초등 초중급 | 전 3 구성

과학·사회·수학 교과서의 핵심 어휘와 개념을 익혀서
논픽션 글감을 이해하는 기초를 쌓습니다.

초등 초중급 | 전 2권 구성

기적의 외국어 학습서

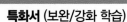

	기본서 (필수 학습)	특화서 (보완/강화 학습)
유아 종합	만 2세 이상 만 3세 이상 만 5세 이상 만 5세 이상	 3세 이상 전 12권 / 3세 이상 전 12권 / 3세 이상 전 12권 3세 이상
파닉스	만 6세 이상 전 3권 만 7세 이상 전 3권	1~3학년
단어	5학년 이상 전 1권	1~3학년
읽기	30 7세~1학년 전 3권  50 2, 3학년 전 3권 / 80 4, 5학년 전 3권 / 120 6학년 이상 전 3권	1~3학년 전 3권
영작	4학년 이상 전 5권 5학년 이상 전 2권	3학년 이상 4, 5학년 5, 6학년 5학년 이상
문법	2학년 이상 전 5권 5학년 이상 전 3권	기적의 동사 변화 트레이닝 6학년 / 기적의 맨처음 영문법 출간 예정
회화 듣기	기적의 영어 듣기 출간 예정	3학년 이상 전 2권